90 DAYS OF FAILURE AND SOME SUCCESS

Praise for Brandon Ficara

"Brandon Ficara possesses an innate wisdom most of us wish we had–the ability to cut through the clutter and find the quickest route to a goal. I have had the privilege of being coached by Brandon and have seen the results firsthand in my business. Serious business development professionals that heed his counsel will reap the benefits."

–Maris Moon: Managing Director Douglas Elliman Property Management

"Brandon Ficara is the somewhat rare sales professional who sees sales as a science, and not just an art. He's always had a remarkable ability to identify future stars very early on in the process, to get them trained properly, and most importantly, to get them through the inevitable slumps. *90 Days of Failure* is written in true Ficarian style. He gets his point out to you right away, with relevant examples and a solid dose of humor and dry wit. The lessons contained here are not only relevant for sales career transitions, but for career transitions in most any field. On more than one occasion, thinking about my decidedly non-sales-related career, I identified concepts and approaches that would have been very helpful to me when undergoing transitions. Brandon has written a very important guide to help people through something that they will almost inevitably experience in their careers."

–Norm Rosenberg: CFO Ambulnz

"Having seen first hand the effect of Brandon's philosophy and guidance for well over a decade, I feel the need to insist that you must read...embrace...and reteach the contents of this book to anyone whose mindset and career you wish to positively impact. "

-Brad Basmajian: Chief Operating Officer Toco Warranty

90 DAYS OF FAILURE AND SOME SUCCESS

Real Life Strategies for Surviving Sales Career Transitions

BRANDON FICARA

Maverick Vision
PUBLISHING

Copyright © 2020 by Brandon Ficara

Cover Copyright ©2020 by Brandon Ficara

Cover Design by Stacey Smekofske

Edited by Dawn Papandrea

Formatting: Stacey Smekofske EditsByStacey.com

ISBNs Print Copy: Paperback 978-1-949318-45-6

Hardcover 978-1-949318-44-9

Digital 978-1-949318-52-4

Published by: Maverick Vision Publishing

I dedicate this book to the person who never loses faith in me, even when I have doubts. To my dearest wife, Andy, I can handle any transition life throws at me as long as you are by my side.

Contents

Introduction

During the writing of this book, the COVID-19 pandemic spread throughout the world. While the world-changing event is still underway as of this book's publication, it has not invalidated any of the strategies, tips and thoughts contained herein. In fact, the pandemic has amplified the need for this book by forcing millions of people out of their jobs due to the economic fallout caused by state and city lockdowns. My hope is that the thoughts and lessons you are about to read will not only provide real-world applicable tools to assist you, but also let you know that you are not alone. We got this!

Transitions are tough. Just think back to when you were a kid and started a new school, the first year of living with another person and all of their quirks, or those first few weeks of becoming a new parent to a screaming mini human. And those examples are the things you saw coming and had time to plan ahead for!

When it comes to your career, many times transitions are forced, unexpected, or ventured into out of necessity or financial pressure. Now here comes the obligatory eye-opening stat that you'd expect to find in a book such as this: **The average person will go through about 10 transitions into new jobs over the course of their**

working lives. And that's not counting transitions into new roles that happen when you stay with one company for an extended period of time.

Each time you head into a transition, those first 90 days into unknown territory are critical. Will you survive? Will you crash and burn? Will you realize you made a terrible mistake and have to crawl back to your old life with your tail between your legs? The truth is that you will succeed (eventually), but first you will fail (miserably).

I should know... I've been there, done that–many times over!

I've gone from aspiring stand-up comedian, to restaurant worker/aspiring actor, to inexperienced call center representative working to keep the lights on, to successful salesperson, to coaching hundreds of people as a talent development sales manager.

When I started thinking back on all of the emotions and fears that I felt during each of my own career transitions (there have been at least four major ones, which you'll learn about later), as well as what it's been like helping hundreds of others navigate transitions of their own, I recognized some common themes.

No, I won't tell you what they are just yet... they will be revealed throughout the book. But before we get to the nitty gritty of transitions, I should tell you a little bit about myself and my background, and why on Earth you should take my transition advice to heart.

A Life in Transition

I was born in Philadelphia in 1975, but grew up in Ocean City, NJ. Both of my parents worked at the Sands Casino, so I grew up watching great comedians like Jerry Seinfeld, Howie Mandel, and Billy Crystal. So, naturally, my dream was to become a stand-up comedian.

I left New Jersey when I was 21 years old and moved to Charleston, South Carolina to do stand-up; to pay the bills, I waited tables. I performed at a lot of great places, and eventually went back to Philly, and then New York. At that point, my comedy career started to stall. So, I did what most aspiring young entertainers do: I moved to Los

Angeles to see if I could launch a different type of entertainment career as an actor.

I was fortunate that I was hired to do some commercials and promo work for MTV, and I also had a guest starring role on the TV show, *My Name is Earl* on NBC. But there was still that rent that needed to be paid as I was hopping from gig to gig, and I had grown tired of waiting tables and working in the food industry. The tricky thing was I needed something with flexible hours that also had the potential to bring in some real income. I went on Craigslist and saw a listing for a part-time sales job in a call center. It looked like it fit what I was looking for, and despite never really selling anything in my life, I applied and got the job.

After the first day of training, I realized I didn't know anything about sales or the products I'd be selling. I was really hoping that it would work out, but the training wasn't very robust. With no mock sales practical testing, I was set loose to figure it out on my own. I was lucky that I had so much experience as a comedian and an entertainer, so I was used to working against odds that were stacked against me. More important, I had an unreasonable and delusional level of self-confidence.

All of that helped me to kill it out of the gate. I had eight sales in three days, and there was some buzz about me quickly becoming the superstar of the office. That, of course, was short-lived. My lack of training caught up with me, so when I would start to run into problems, I didn't have the necessary tools to navigate them. Plus, my manager was, shall we say, less than helpful. In fact, he was a total jerk who berated me for doing what I was told to do. I was ready to give up. It was the first major crossroads of my sales career, and it was as rocky as it gets. I was literally within minutes of it being over at any point.

Spoiler alert: I made a decision right then and there to take full ownership of my career, and despite some big learning curves, I was able to get through my first, very shaky sales transition. It's a good thing, too, because as I kept going back to sales in between acting jobs, I realized that I was starting to fall in love with it. Acting wasn't bringing me a whole lot of joy. And though I still loved stand-up, it was sales that was becoming a bigger part of my life. A few years into it, I had my first opportunity in sales management, and that's when the real lightbulb went off.

I found it far more rewarding to be able to influence other sales-people on how to attain their goals and get them to perform at a higher level. Over the years, I saw a lot of people come and go, and made career leaps of my own—all of that gave me some great insights into what it's like to transition. Not to mention the fact that I lived in the motherland of transition—Los Angeles, the place where so many people move to without a real game plan and then suddenly realize they have to figure things out. Although I didn't know it when I was the one figuring things out in L.A. for the first time, transition would become a recurring theme in my life.

When I tried to explore that idea some more, I realized that there haven't been a whole lot of seminars or books about the topic, so I made another important transition in my life. I went from the mindset that "*Someone* should write about this," to "*I'm* going to write about this." And so, here we are.

What you have in your hands is not just an ordinary sales book...

It's the guide that I wish I had when I headed into tough transitions with absolutely no clue as to how I was going to make it work. This book will walk you through that critical 90-day transitional period as you get started in a new career opportunity.

You'll learn, among other things:

- Why transitions happen
- The stages of transition
- How to be confident during transition
- Why training is so important for transition success
- How to navigate the sales environment the first 90 days
- Strategies for getting over the first sales slump

- How to stay passionate about your job
- How to cement strong habits

Along the way, I'll share anecdotes about the many people who have gotten it right, as well as what went wrong for those who could have used a book like this to help navigate their transitions better.

The fact is most of the sales professionals I have encountered have been extremely talented. So why didn't they all succeed? One of the biggest reasons is that they weren't equipped to handle those initial 90 days on the job in a way that set them up for success.

Why Is This Book Worthy of Your Time?

The reality is that career transition is an inevitable part of your journey. The vast majority of people don't stay in one career or with one company forever, and even for those who do, there is often a lot of shifting, adapting, and evolving that needs to happen in order to keep up with company changes, industry trends, and new technologies.

Consider this:

- In January 2016, the Bureau of Labor Statistics reported the average employee tenure was 4.2 years, down from 4.6 years in January 2014. That comes to just about 10 transitions for someone whose career spans from age 22 to 65.
- Seventy-six percent of workers ages 35 to 39 had an average job duration of fewer than five years.

In other words, the ability to transition is one of the most important skill sets you'll need. Without it, your career will suffer. I've met many people who are downright aggressive in their opposition to change. That mindset can be limiting if you are in a position to control your environment; or it can be devastating if your career finds itself in a transition that is beyond your control.

It's my hope that this book will help you be ready for your next transition–big or small–so that you're not left behind.

How to Get the Most of This Book

For me, this book was years in the making. It's the collective wisdom of my personal and professional experiences, and the consolidation of some of the proven strategies that I've used to help countless salespeople surpass their goals. But while I put a lot of thought into how to use transitional periods as launching pads to reach the next level of your career development, just passively skimming through my thoughts isn't going to help you.

Here's what will:

Mental preparation. Think about how teams huddle together before a game, or how performers close their eyes and take a deep breath right before they walk on stage. To mentally prepare yourself to dive into this book, take a moment to think about where you are in your career right now, and where you think it might be heading. Or perhaps you might reflect on a time that your career trajectory didn't go the way you'd hoped. With a more focused mindset, even if you're not in the midst of a transition right now, you'll find useful takeaways from the stories and exercises.

Bringing the right attitude. Just as I'll allude to many times in this book, thinking you've already learned all there is to know is not going to set you up for success. I've met tons of salespeople who were top notch, but who completely melted down over changes in process, or having to adapt to a new system. That's why it's crucial that you approach this guide–or any sales strategy advice–with an open mind. Sure, some of the advice may not be applicable to your current situation, or you might think that you've handled past transitions like a boss. But trust me–even situations that start off great can become scary real fast. I can tell you that it was those times in my life that I admitted to myself that I didn't know enough, and then reached out for help and guidance, that I was able to push past plateaus and grow.

Approaching this book as a participatory activity. Look, I can sit here and say that if you read my book, it will be life altering, but that's not really true. You have to do the work. That's why I decided to add **"Get-to-Work" Worksheets** at the end of each chapter. Do the exercises. I promise, they'll get you thinking about your personal career development and help you perform some honest self-assessment.

So now that you know who I am, why I wrote this book, and what it could do for you, it's time to jump in. Your sales career transition education begins in 3, 2, 1...

Preparing For The Transition

In my other life as a stand-up comedian, there is a moment right before I take the stage that I have to put my *game face* on. I'm trying to remember what I am going to say, get fired up to meet the crowd with confidence and energy, tuck all of my fears and insecurities into the dark reaches of my psyche, and finally remind myself that what I am about to experience is a gift. As you begin this journey, remember that no matter why you are at this juncture, it is a gift just to be able to begin the journey...oh, and be sure to pee first, it will make the whole thing more enjoyable.

ONE

Why the Transition

EVERY TRANSITION IS DIFFERENT. Some are planned, some aren't; some happen because of external factors while others are a personal choice.

Before learning coping strategies, it's important to understand why transitions happen in the first place. This chapter will go over the different factors, both internal and external that will contribute to a need or desire to transition to a new job or new role.

Another way of thinking about internal versus external factors, is whether your transition is volitional or thrust upon you.

A *volitional* cause might be that you're not satisfied with the job you're in currently, and decide you'd like to try a new industry or product. A *non-volitional* reason would be something like the company you're working for goes out of business. Both can be scary propositions, but both can be handled in a way that puts you in a better situation than before. That is, if you apply a little bit of care, effort and thought.

Here's a look at some of the most common transition scenarios and their causes:

Internal Factors

When you're motivated to make a transition in your sales career because something is happening in your own life, regardless of the business or industry you're in, that's an internal factor. Here are a few of the most common ones:

1. **You want a better work life balance.** Sometimes a simple and common reason for making a transition is that you're stressed to the max. Car sales is a great example. In order to really get ahead, you have to work 10-12 hours, constantly be on your feet, and work weekends and holidays. Beyond the physical stress, there's possibly some impact on your relationships. Whatever the reason, sometimes people decide they need to look for a lighter schedule. It's not that they're lazy–everyone has different definitions of what they consider to be success in their lives. As you move forward, you realize that true success is having a balance of feeling content within your home as well as outside of it. In your relationships, physically, mentally, spiritually, and financially. A lot of people in more demanding fields of sales will find themselves at some point willing to make a little less money to have more balance. Yes, this realization can bring with it feelings of guilt, anxiety, and inadequacy because your internal bully will protest the idea of not spending every waking moment grinding for more sales and greater wealth. The idea of slowing down can feel a lot like giving up because you can't handle the pressures of the job. While this notion is objectively false, it can create an emotional dilemma that can make transitioning a challenge.

2. **Your family is expanding.** Gone are the days of it being the norm for dad to work all day and come home where the kids are given instructions to not bother dad because he's had a long day. For the most part, we live in a two-income society in which both mom and dad want to contribute to the family not just as financial providers, but

with their time and care. It's a positive for society as a whole but is often the cause of career transitions. That's because once you become a parent, the responsibility level in the home goes up, and you may have a strong desire to want to be a little more plugged in to your family's life. While this is perhaps the most understandable and noble cause for a career transition, it can be a big challenge to master two new roles at once. The pressures (and sleeplessness) of parenting can't easily be turned off as you try to simultaneously get up to speed during a change in your career.

3. **You are faced with your own physical limitation or illness, or that of someone in your family.** If you've ever been in the position of being a caregiver, you know how challenging that can be to feel like you're not fulfilling your responsibilities at your job or doing enough to take care of your family when they need you most. It's like you're being stretched in two different directions, and in many cases, you might have to transition your role or find a new line of work that gives you the kind of flexibility needed to take care of the people you love. Maintaining focus and keeping your emotions in check while navigating a physical and emotionally draining reality can be overwhelming. You may feel like you are doing a lousy job as a caregiver *and* in your new role. If you find yourself dealing with a new illness or injury, whether it's seen or unseen, you may also have to make adjustments in your career so you can recover or cope. Feeling physically diminished or not on top of your game, even temporarily, can further complicate the demands of a career transition.

4. **You are offered a new or expanded role.** A lot of times in sales, the better you do, the more spotlight the company shines on you. From your perspective, someone wants to screw up all the great money you're making in the anonymity of your comfort zone by giving you more

responsibility. But really, it's because they want your example to permeate through the organization. So, you're asked to take on more of a leadership role in the company. Aside from the drag it can be for a new position to get in the way of your perfect workflow and feeling great about being on top of the sales board, there is a lot of gratification that can go along with such growth. Along with that higher purpose within the organization, there is a whole new set of skills to learn. Of course, from a skill perspective, it's like going back to being a newbie again. When you've been a dominant sales force in your company, it can be challenging to go back to being a learner again. *(We'll get into this more in Chapter 4.)*

5. **Your job sucks and you've had enough.** Why do people stay in jobs that suck for years while telling everybody who will listen that their job sucks? Well, look, a lot of why people stay in a job is that they are afraid of the unknown. Not only are they afraid of what a new opportunity will be, but they're afraid of that transitional period–afraid to be new again. Even though the reality is they sit in the parking lot for an extra 20 minutes because they have to work up the energy to walk in, and they drink alcohol to erase the memory of the horrible day they had. They keep going back because there's a comfort level in the status quo. Moving on means having to worry: *"What if I'm not the top salesperson? What if I don't have some of the comforts I've come to expect from a job?"* Later in the book, I'll not only share strategies on how to pick the right job for you, but you'll become equipped to handle that transition so you can feel confident and excited to tackle something new.

Whether your internal factors are positive or negative, the good news is with the proper approach, you can not only transition to a new normal in your life, but you can prosper. I've witnessed many people having to leave something they were excellent at, and they end up taking a job for which the transition is extremely difficult. But once things settle, they have put themselves in a position to flourish even more than they would have in their previous reality.

External Factors

Sometimes, the world is thrust upon you and you have no choice but to make a transition. This is the result of external factors that you have no control over, and they can create a very uncomfortable situation, especially if you're happy in your work. Here are some of the common ones that you may experience:

1. **Business closure and layoff.** I've been there a couple of times. In a lot of cases, there may be a lead up or warning signs. Some of you might be reading this book right now because you know that in a month, you might be out of a job, so this is a great time to dive in. Other times, these changes happen without warning, and you're forced to figure things out and transition quickly amidst feelings of shock and anger. Your new employer may be sympathetic to how your last situation ended, but they bear no responsibility for making it better. In this case, you are the only person with the power to let go of past events, no matter how recent, so you can make the most of this new opportunity. It can be challenging to come back from a gut punch like that, but believe me, it can be done.

2. **Changes in the industry.** Listen, we live in the digital age, and it's hard to find an industry that has not been disrupted. In fact, many sales professionals will tell you that they live in a constant state of flux. Some examples in the sales world might be moving from the physical space to the online space. That might put you in a position where in order to make the living you're used to you have to change and adapt. You have to transition into a new job

either inside or outside of your company. Disruption is a big buzz word that means growth in an industry, and usually good things for customers, but a lot of times there could be negative fallout for the people who were used to making their living a certain way. But that's a transition that a lot of people have to make. You need to mourn quickly, or you could fail to make the transition a successful one. Nostalgia is not your friend here. In the immortal words of Billy Joel, *"The good old days weren't always good, and tomorrow ain't as bad as it seems."* Over the next 15-20 years, it will happen at an even faster rate as more things move online, and marketing changes how the company interacts with the customer.

3. **New products.** Sometimes it happens that you're in the same job, but your company decides to throw you a curve ball and totally change up its product line. This happens a lot in pharmaceutical and medical technology companies, or sometimes things change due to new regulations or ways of doing business. This can leave the most experienced salesperson in a position they haven't been in for quite some time—where they don't know what they're talking about or are not as confident about the products they're selling. It can be extremely challenging depending on where you are in your career, how well you mastered the previous product line, and what's being asked of you. For example, in pharmaceutical sales, your relationships with doctors are the most important thing you have. You have built them over time, and you've earned your customers' trust. Now if your company changes from one kind of product to another, it could mean you have to sell to a whole new specialty of doctors and you're back to square one. Now you're meeting new doctors who don't know you, who might not want to give you the time of day. It might not seem like a major factor compared to some of the above but tell that to someone who had their entire

territory or product line changed. But there is some great news–it's going to be an opportunity to be in a better spot than you were. If you can navigate that transition (and hopefully this book can help), you'll end up in a position where you're back on top again faster than you would have been.

Wild Card: Relocation

This particular type of transition can be internal (you're moving to be closer to family) or external (your company is relocating you). Either way, you are facing all of the same challenges as with any transition, as well as having to restart your life in an unfamiliar setting. While there is the inherent excitement when you arrive in a new place that's ripe with possibilities, there's also social, personal, and economic uncertainty that comes with it. Will you make friends and establish a support system easily? Where the hell are you going to live? Will this new place have your favorite kind of ice cream at the supermarket? All of these questions have answers (and you might even discover a new favorite dessert!). You'll figure it out, and even if this isn't going to be your forever location, you can make the transition successfully. It's important to remember that no door locks behind you when you move. Learning that a new place isn't right for you isn't a failure, but not giving it a real chance is.

If you are in one of these situations and reading this book, be open to the fact that even though your life is more of a challenge than it was yesterday, that doesn't mean you can't find yourself in a happier, more productive place. Even if the world seems like it turned upside on you and you feel the weight of it, know that it will continue to spin, and eventually you'll be right back on top.

Degrees of Transition

A transition can have different degrees of impact on you. Some are slight such as a simple change of schedule. You might have the same job, same product, same platform, but instead of working traditional hours, you have to work a different shift. That's one end of the spectrum. On the other side, maybe you go from a call center to face-to-face sales. Or selling tangible products in one format to selling an intangible product in another format. Another big one is the transition from B2C (business to consumer) to B2B (business to business). Those would be considered bigger transitions.

Either way, I'm here to tell you that size really doesn't matter. Yes, there are many degrees of transition, but there's also many different degrees of how people handle their transitions. There are many examples of people who made a monumental transition, but they totally rolled with it and it didn't create a lot of turmoil for them–even though what they were doing was completely different. On the flipside, you might have someone who makes a simple switch and their sales numbers and confidence plummet, putting them on the brink of having to find a new job.

So, understand this: While there are different degrees of transition, your attitude and what you bring to the table is going to have more of an impact to your success than the nature of the transition itself. I've seen it firsthand where people have literally spiraled out of control and fallen apart with even the smallest tweaks, while others have made monumental leaps without missing a beat.

The fact that you have this book in front of you says you're approaching your own change in a very healthy way. You're looking for strategies. You're acknowledging that a transition is happening (or about to happen) and you're taking a proactive approach to being successful.

Transitions take work and effort no matter what. But your attitude is what's going to play a huge role in how big your transition feels–regardless of how big it actually is!

Meet John, the Transition Resistor

John, a top salesman I managed, was very happy with his job and made great money. He worked a morning shift, usually 7 a.m. to 3 p.m. and things were going great. But his daughter was starting preschool and his wife's work circumstances changed, leaving a gap as to who could get their child off to school in the morning. John knew our company would be happy to work with him, and so he changed his hours to 1 p.m. to 9 p.m., so he could get his daughter ready for school. It seemed like it should be an easy transition since it was just a time change.

He had a rough first week, but since he was a consistent performer, no one thought much of it. We saw it as just getting used to the new schedule and dealing with the emotions of preschool drop-off. (Hint: It's not easy if you've never done it!) In the second week, it was more of the same. He was getting frustrated because he was selling aggressively but was still not getting results. This continued for the next three weeks. His numbers were falling-off-a-cliff bad.

He'd been meeting with his direct manager, who reported to me, and I thought it was about time for John and me to sit down face to face. I started by asking him, "Why don't you tell me what you've been experiencing?" He told me he was doing everything the same as he was before, and he felt like he was working hard, and his metrics backed that up. But the customers were just not saying yes. He said he was doing everything in his power to influence them and talk about products and using the sales process and it just wasn't working.

After hearing him out, I said, "Let me ask you this. When you came into work today, how did you feel getting started?" He said he was frustrated. I empathized, and said, "You are doing everything you're supposed to do, but what would you *like* to do?" And then he let loose. He said he'd like to wake up, take a shower, get dressed, pick up a coffee, and get right in and go after his book and put up early sales to set the tone for the day—like he used to. Instead, he wakes up and spends the next hour trying to wrangle his daughter, but he feels like he's not doing it well. She's always crying at drop-off, melting down in front of other parents. He felt like he'd already had a full day by the time he walked into work, and only to get kicked in the face with a bunch of rejection from customers.

So that was John's perspective dealing with what might seem like one of the lightest and easiest types of transitions. Had he forgotten how to sell? No. But he was feeling unsuccessful in the rest of his life. His real transition was having to get his kid fed, dressed, and off to school. In hearing his frustration, it became evident that when you don't feel like you're successful in another area of your life, it can have a tremendous impact in your confidence level, and a tremendous impact in your results. I wasn't coaching him on sales, I was coaching him on managing his expectations on what a 3-year-old was capable of. He needed to learn how to be more patient so he could be a more successful parent, a more successful partner to his wife, and he can come into work more confident. "You don't need help in sales, you need help with everything else," I told him. "You may be feeling some resentment, but you have to let that go."

After a brief laugh, he conceded that he was having difficulty adjusting to his new hands-on role of taking care of his daughter in the mornings. He felt like a failure and resented his wife for "Putting him in that position." Trying to be supportive, I agreed that she must have it in for him to disrupt his perfect situation. He laughed again and the light bulb went off. "She didn't have a choice–I do." He continued, "I just feel like a failure. Why is it so hard for me to get this kid to go along with the program?" I responded, "It's new for her, too." Lightbulb number two! "She's three years old, she's supposed to be a baby, what's my excuse?" he said with a smile of understanding.

I coached him about learning how to get in a rhythm where you can get your child off to preschool and feel good about it. And over time, that's what he did. He started to see an uptick in sales as he improved his real transition to get his child off to school.

Real Life Lesson

John was able to be successful, but he made it harder than it needed to be in the beginning because he resisted the change. He liked his old schedule and he didn't like the fact that he had to change it, so he resisted it. When you start from a place of resistance, you allow mole hills to turn into mountains. Once the resistance stopped and he started looking for solutions, things got easier. Today, John is still in that schedule and still a top performer who's doing well for himself.

So that's an example of how to take a minor transition and make it as difficult as possible. So thanks, John, for taking one for the team and presenting us with that example.

Meet Maggie, the Proactive Transitioner

Now let's look at a big transition–going from B2C call center sales to B2B service sales. Maggie was working B2C but got to a point where she felt she had been doing the same thing for 15 years and wanted a change. She thought she could bring more value to a company doing B2B sales. Because of the internal factor of wanting or needing a change, she took a big leap to a software product company that required things she was not accustomed to. She wouldn't be starting out with a book of business, but instead, prospecting and establishing a new territory from scratch. She'd also be dealing with gatekeepers for the first time, and a much longer and more detailed sales process and sales cycle that lasted three to six months. At certain points, it would require collaboration with other people in the organization, and as the sale grew closer, the customer's IT people, and her IT people would have to get together. And all of that would happen *before* there was a sale.

Knowing she would be entering a new industry, in the lead up to going away for 10-day training, she began going on lunch dates with people in similar fields. She wasn't looking for leads, just advice on what it was going to take to be successful. She got to reconnect with people and get tips on sales books, blogs, and industry periodicals that could help her.

During the training, Maggie made it a point to use her evening free time to her advantage. First, she organized a study session with other trainees over a bottle of wine. This helped cement what they learned, but also added a social element. Second, she tried starting relationships not just with trainees, but with others in the organization so she could start to feel like part of a work family.

Real Life Lesson

By spending her transition period wisely, Maggie and her team saw some really early success. While it's never easy making a transition like that, within a short amount of time, their territory was up to speed, and once the sales cycle started coming to fruition, the money was great. She had been happy from day one because of her attitude and her approach. Success wasn't immediate, but it happened in a shorter amount of time than was expected. She took full ownership of her situation, and made sure she understood the challenges ahead, while working on building bonds with her team. She understood that her transition was not going to happen in a vacuum. The people around you are going to either help you or hinder you, and a lot of that will come down to your attitude going in.

Hopefully John's and Maggie's stories help illustrate two things:

1. There are a lot of different degrees of transition
2. The level of ease and smoothness of the transition often has much more to do with you than it does with the size of the transition.

TRANSITIONAL TAKEAWAYS

So far, you've learned there are many different types of sales career transitions, with varying degrees of difficulty. If we didn't cover yours, hopefully there's something close enough to correlate with your experience. To quickly review, here are the important concepts to remember as you move forward in the book:

1. **You're not alone.** Transitions in the sales industry are extremely common and can happen because of a variety of internal and external factors. As such, the people who have gone through them will attest that there is a road map toward success. Not only have they navigated the transition but ended up happier than they were beforehand. So that should be encouraging as you move forward.

2. **Transitions don't last forever.** You want to look at the transition into a new world in sales–whether it's a new industry, company, product, or role–as a singular process that has a beginning, middle, and end. So even though the transition can feel uncomfortable, it does have an end to it. Knowing there is a light at the end of the tunnel should bring you some comfort.

3. **The size of your transition is not as big a determining success factor as your own attitude.** When we fight a transition, no matter what the size (like in John's example) we find we can make a fairly easy one pretty darn hard. And no matter how big the transition, you can make it successful and in record time (like Maggie) by putting in the work and bringing the right attitude to the process.

Final Thought

This book is a tool that will help you, but it's ultimately up to the person holding the book to make the most of it. If I can help move the needle for you by offering a couple of new tricks and tools, I'll have done my job, but that's not going to always guarantee a drama-free transition.

My hope is that you'll be able to look back and say, "I made it through, and this book was a great tool that helped me." But I will tell you this: The fact that you even picked this book up says you are proactive and have the right attitude, and it puts you light years ahead of the majority of people going through transition.

Motivational Mantra:
"No transition is too big for a good attitude."

GET-TO-WORK WORKSHEET

Is a Transition in Your Future?

Exercise 1: Take a moment to really examine how you feel about your current situation. Do you have a positive or negative outlook?

Positive:

- ❑ You feel valued at your job.
- ❑ You've learned at least one thing that's made you better at your job, or picked up a new skill in the last 6 months.
- ❑ You're on a growth trajectory.
- ❑ You have a generally positive outlook about the future of your role, your company, and your industry.
- ❑ You work hard, but you still find time for a healthy personal life.
- ❑ You have mentors and a manager at work who are supportive.

Negative:

- ❑ It takes all of your energy just to walk into the office each day.
- ❑ You feel unappreciated and underpaid.
- ❑ You are just going through the motions, and no longer feel fulfilled at work.
- ❑ You're not confident that your job or company will even exist six months from now.
- ❑ You're comfortable in your job, but it's not conducive to a home life.
- ❑ Your stress levels are through the roof.
- ❑ Your boss and/or colleagues have an "every man for himself" attitude.

Exercise 2: Are there internal or external factors in the works that might bring about a transition for you in the near future?

- ❑ You are dealing with a health crisis or have taken on a caregiving role at home.
- ❑ Your family dynamics are changing.
- ❑ Your company has gone through a round of layoffs recently.
- ❑ Your industry is facing new government regulations.
- ❑ Your company is shifting toward marketing automation and a new sales platform.
- ❑ You're sick of selling the products you've been selling and want a change.
- ❑ Your partner may have to relocate for work, which means you do, too.

TWO

What to Expect When You're Transitioning

As MENTIONED on the first page of this book, transition is tough, but how you ride it out will dictate your success or failure.

This chapter might be a bit of a gut punch, but I assure you, it's for your own good. We just went over a lot of reasons for a transition in your sales career and now we're going to discuss some of the realities that you may experience during your transition. I'm going to be honest—a lot of them are tough and can seem very daunting. But the purpose of this book is to help you, and it's not fair to sugarcoat the things you're going to be dealing with. The last thing I want is for you to say, "This book said transitions would be so easy, but I'm experiencing all these feelings and challenges, so there must be something wrong with me." It's *not* easy. And there's nothing wrong with you.

The reason I'm getting all of the negative stuff out right up front isn't to freak you out. It's for two reasons:

1. I want to be honest with you about what you can expect to experience.
2. I want you to know that you are not the first (or even the millionth!) person to go through this.

I want you to feel the opposite of scared after this chapter. Not only have countless people experienced it, but many have triumphed, and with the right effort on your part, it's almost a guarantee that you will become one of the success stories. The fact that you're reading these words right now is an indication that you are involved in your own success. .

By understanding the challenges that go into this turbulent time in your career and meeting those challenges head on with the right attitude and a good strategy, you're going to be able to come through the other side of the transition and say, "I did it. I did it and I'm in a great place." And *that* is my goal for you, and the goal of this book. In service to that goal, I will be brutally honest with you about what you're going to face.

Let's start by breaking down some of the most common things you will experience on an emotional level so there are no major surprises when you're in the thick of a transition.

Discomfort

If you already have a sinking feeling in the pit of your stomach, hang in there! Help is on the way. Discomfort is as necessary to success as dice are to Yahtzee. You can't run from it. You can't hide from it. Your level of resistance will dictate the duration of your transition.

Why does change have to be uncomfortable? We humans have a way of creating rhythms and cheats in our daily work. Usually, those cheats and rhythms are very specific to the success of the current job that you have. When you transition within your company to a new role or to a new company entirely, your cheats no longer apply. You must think about each task, continually fretting over the quality of your new work. Why do some continue to use the tools that were more comfortable in their last job no matter how inefficient they are in their new environment? The excuse you will often hear is that it is faster to do it the old way that is easier.

Meet Rob, the Reluctant Resistor

Rob was a new salesperson that I trained and managed at a specialty insurance firm. We ran into a little issue when he insisted on using Outlook to set his sales appointments instead of using the fully integrated CRM (customer relationship management) platform that logs calls and sets follow-up tasks automatically. He was unequivocal that it was faster for him to stick with his faithful Outlook calendar.

Having witnessed this resistance to change more times than I can count, I knew that forcing adoption would create even more resistance. I recommended using the expensive tools he was being provided one last time but left the choice up to him. Truth be told, Rob's way was faster initially. He was setting appointments faster than the other three members of the training group who bought into the CRM in all of its glory, but who had a learning curve to get through. By day two, however, the others were up to speed and by day three, my stubborn friend was falling behind and less organized than the others. He was toggling back and forth between screens trying to keep up.

Lesson Learned

If you fail to embrace the discomfort of change you might get away with the more comfortable path for a brief moment. But beyond that, actively resisting could cause more harm than good. Although he eventually began using the CRM, he made a simple transition harder than it had to be. Lucky for Rob, his example is fairly benign as there was no big consequence of a result of his discomfort, just a small bump in the road.

Meet Jackie, the Bad Habit Boomerang

What happens when the behavior isn't a simple productivity tool, but a process that is crucial to your success? If you resist a sales process that is tailor made for your industry or to align with compliance procedures that are legally necessary, you might be letting your discomfort lead to flaming out of your new job after a couple of painful months.

That's what happened with Jackie. When I interviewed her, she couldn't tell me enough how *done* she was with the industry from which she was transitioning. She was a top seller for over 10 years but had grown tired of the politics and selling practices. She went into great detail to outline every part of the industry that didn't agree with her, even circling back to make sure she hadn't missed anything.

Despite her eagerness for something different, in training, I noticed she wasn't following our sales process. She wasn't being defiant; she was actually quite pleasant. But she simply couldn't stop using the very approach that she had seemed downright jubilant to abandon when she was hired. After a few days, I let her know that she wouldn't be able to exit training if she wasn't executing our process. She agreed and muscled through the training, exiting with a pretty good test score.

But guess what? As soon as she began talking to clients, she immediately reverted to her old way of selling. It just didn't work, and after numerous coaching sessions and 90 agonizing days, we parted ways.

Real Life Lesson

What do you think Jackie did next? You guessed it–she went right back to the industry that she left. Her transition didn't fail because she couldn't do the job. She failed because she simply couldn't cope with the discomfort of change.

Growth

The second thing that will always accompany change is growth. While everyone agrees that growth is a good thing, it requires a certain degree of humility to reap the full

benefits. But for salespeople, it's in their nature to be a little over-confident. Think about it: If you are going to climb the unclimbable mountain and make a sale that no one has ever been able to close, then you have to be a bit delusional with respect to your own talent and readiness. Those that can harness this mild form of insanity can achieve amazing results. But during times of change, you have to be able to check your ego at the door–and that can be hard to do.

In other words, the very attribute that makes you a successful salesperson–your confidence–might become an obstacle when you're in a transition period. If you see yourself as being nearly perfect, that can make it difficult to identify areas that need improvement within your new environment–or even admit that you need improvement at all.

As someone who has witnessed this happen hundreds of times, I can pretty easily spot the signs of someone who's letting their ego get in the way of their growth. For instance, a new hire from a different industry resists coaching and progress meetings. Another big clue is hearing the dreaded phrase, "I know." When all of my training and instruction is met with "I know," all I can think is, "No. You don't."

In order to grow and be successful with your new job, product, or process, you must start from the position that you don't know everything. From there, follow this change action plan:

- **Envision your success after the change.** Keeping this image in your mind will help propel you through uncomfortable growing pains.
- **Make a list of skills to develop.** Now that you accept that you don't know everything, what do you need to learn to master your next role?
- **Define goals with the help of management.** Ask others who are already successful for their input on the necessary skills that help them thrive.
- **Partner with your new manager on feedback cadence.** Utilize sales management and talent development as partners to shepherd you through the change and clearly

define your outcome. Being proactive with your manager will make coaching less about what you did wrong, and more about tracking your success.

- **Don't take yourself too seriously.** Laugh when you fall on your face trying something new. Ask "Why?" even when you want to protect your ego with an "I know." Trust that you will be a top performer soon and every bit of discomfort will be rewarded with breakaway success.

Change is difficult, but it can be a great source of pride when you make the adjustment successfully.

Financial Pressure

In addition to the general feeling of discomfort of being new and having to figure it out, there's that other big stressor that accompanies most transitions (most notably in sales), and that's financial pressure.

As we stated in Maggie's story in the last chapter, she was able to build her book of business rather quickly, but it didn't happen overnight. She understood that there would be some financial sacrifices while she transitioned into her new role. In most sales jobs, it takes some time to build a pipeline, and during that period, your income is the lowest it's ever going to be. Along with being new and figuring things out, it's a one-two punch that can make transitions more stressful

In a perfect world, you'll already have some money socked away in an emergency fund to cover your expenses as your income ramps back up. But if the transition took you by surprise or you are not in a great financial position–and that's probably the more likely scenario–you will still be OK if you take a smart approach.

First off, you have to get firm hold on your budget and make temporary decisions to ease your financial discomfort. In most cases, when we sacrifice a little bit up front, the rewards afterward are more bountiful. The best way to survive and get through lean times is to develop a strong plan based on your situation and set a timeline that allows you to see light at the end of the tunnel.

Here are some strategies to keep in mind:

- **Don't avoid the mail.** A lot of times when there's financial pressure, we don't even want to open up our bills. Instead, if you're struggling, reach out to your account providers and make a plan with them. Talk to them up front before payments are past due. Explain that you're transitioning jobs, and in most cases, they may be able to set you up with a payment plan.
- **Cut down on wants.** What do you really need? Probably not Netflix, Hulu, and Amazon Prime. And do you need that gym membership you're barely using? Sometimes when we run into financial pressure, we can make that pressure more manageable by eliminating the fluff in our lives for a short period of time. You work hard and deserve nice things, but you also have to be realistic about your situation. Do yourself a favor and cut your bills down as lean as you can to reduce the financial pressure.
- **Get on a budget.** Do you really know where all those hard-earned dollars are going? If you don't already have a budget, it's time to create one. Add up all of your fixed expenses and estimate your other spending (you'll probably need to track spending for a few days to get a sense of how your typical purchases add up). Your goal should always be to have more than enough income to cover the total. Work it out on paper, using a spreadsheet, or using apps like Mint. *(See budget worksheet at the end of the chapter.)*

Guilt

Whenever you put all of your focus on a new endeavor, it can create a lot of feelings of guilt because you might be taking time away from your personal life. We have families, relationships, and people who count on us for support, and during your transition, you might not be able to fulfill those obligations to the same degree–hence, why you may feel overcome with guilt.

It's hard to look your 8-year-old in the face and say, "Daddy can't come to your baseball game because I have to study product material so I can be ready for work on Monday." Your bowling league might have to get by without you for a season. And your new spouse will eat dinner alone some nights. But those are the kinds of shared sacrifices you and your support team have to be prepared to make.

Even if you push away the guilt, what often happens is that when you run into obstacles in your transition, you'll start asking yourself, "What am I even doing this for?" or "Why am I sacrificing all this, just to fall on my face?" The reality is that in any transition there's always going to be some level of doubt. Just remember this: The reason you're doing it is because you are talented enough, ambitious enough, and motivated enough to create the life that you want. And, the sacrifices you're making today are temporary, but can have a positive impact on your family for years to come.

Mourning

Whether you're leaving a position voluntarily or because of outside factors, there will be elements of your past life that you will miss. Whether it's relationships, the deli next to the office, the schedule you had, or a mentor you're leaving behind, there will be feelings of loss when you transition. And when you experience a loss, you will want to mourn.

The key is to remind yourself that just because things are changing, doesn't mean you have to give up your old life in its entirety. You might miss your old colleagues, but you'll just have to work a little harder to keep in touch. It can be done. These people are still in your world, just maybe not in your immediate everyday world.

Similar to guilt, feelings of loss will feel stronger whenever you encounter any difficulties during your transition. The grass is greener on the other side has never been truer than when you're feeling challenged or stressed in a new situation. You tend to remember the old gig in sepia tones and wonder, "Maybe I should just go back?"

Some people do go back, and that's OK. But once you've made the decision to try something new, it's best if you at least get through the transition period so you can see what the new world looks like before you do an about-face. You'll never know during a transition if the new situation is going to be better or worse, so you owe it to yourself to get through the transition as quickly as you can. Only then can you accurately assess the new opportunity so you can make an intelligent decision about your next moves instead of an emotional one.

TRANSITIONAL TAKEAWAYS

The biggest takeaway for this chapter is growth. Yes, there is going to be discomfort and we talked about the different types of discomfort extensively because we want you to be prepared. But growth is a commodity. It actually has a monetary value attached to it. So, whether you decided to make a change in your career, or one was thrust upon you, you will be stagnant no more. You might not like the feeling of getting knocked out of your comfort zone at first, but with that, your growth is inevitable.

You can't get out of growth's way right now. You're going to build skills. You're going to harden your resolve. You're going to grow intellectually. And all of these things will make you a more viable candidate in the sales world.

So, yes, there is discomfort, but don't lose sight of the growth. The growth is what will make it possible for you to keep making transitions and advance your career. Maybe you're not used to being a leader and that's what's being asked of you. You're going to have to grow. But by growing you're going to learn skills, become proficient in those skills, and hopefully become an expert in those skills. And *that* will put you in a position to make gains in the quality of your career, as well as in the number on your paycheck.

So, get excited for the growth, because once you've grown, you'll be more valuable. The very nature of transition is that you're in a situation in which you *must* grow. In other words, your value is about to go up and that's pretty exciting.

This has been a cornerstone of my own career thus far. I've had a willingness to transition to different roles and I've had to swallow mega-tons of my own ego. I've fallen on my face and had abysmal failures in certain areas, but man, I've grown from each and every one of those experiences.

In retrospect, some things could be labeled as a misstep or wrong move in my career, but (excuse the cliché) I wouldn't change any of them because that's what has gotten me here. I've transitioned my way to this point in time in which I believe I know enough about this subject to help you as you go through your journey.

Best of all, now that all of the negatives are out of the way, it's time to get excited. Sharpen those pencils–the real work is about to begin!

Motivational Mantra:
"I accept discomfort as a necessary component for my growth."

GET-TO-WORK WORKSHEETS

Exercise 1: Identify the potential discomfort you might face in order to experience growth.

- ❏ I am the breadwinner of the family, so we'd have to make financial sacrifices.

- ❏ I really love my current job and feel afraid that I'm giving up my happiness for the unknown.

- ❏ I'd need my partner to pick up the slack at home, and I'm worried that it might cause a strain in our relationship.

- ❏ It's hard to start back at square one when I'm used to being at the top of my game.

- ❏ I don't know if I have the right skills to handle this transition, and worry that I'll make a mistake.

- ❏ I have to temporarily give up a hobby or interest that is important to me.

Exercise 2: Now that you've identified potential challenges, what are some of the benefits you hope to achieve?

- ❏ Even though I'm taking a risk, I'll develop new skills that I can apply no matter how things end up.

- ❏ I've been comfortable for a while, but it's time to move the needle on my career.

- ❏ My industry is changing, so transitioning to this new role will help give me job security.

- ❏ My family is supportive, and understands that putting in the work up front will allow for better work life balance later.

- ❏ Starting something new is scary, but I haven't been this excited in a long time.

- ❏ I'll have a stronger personal brand and be more valuable to more employers once I've conquered these hurdles.

Exercise 3: Your 5-Minute Budget

1. Calculate all of your monthly fixed expenses.
These are your monthly bills that are generally the same each month, and that you must pay.

Housing costs
Mortgage/rent $_____
Utility bills (gas/electric) $_____

Technology
Mobile phone $_____
Internet $_____
Cable $_____

Transportation
Auto finance/lease payment $_____
Car insurance $_____
Gas $_____

Tolls/parking $_____

Childcare/education (if applicable)
Daycare $_____
School tuition $_____

Personal debt (if applicable)
Student loans $_____
Credit cards (minimum payment) $_____

2. Estimate remaining expenses.

These are items that you spend money on monthly, but there is some flexibility and fluctuation. Look back on the past couple of months to see what you typically spend on these items. This will help you choose an amount for your budget. Even better, these are areas you can potentially cut down when your income decreases.

Groceries

Food $ _____

Household supplies $ _____

Savings $ _____

Emergency fund

Retirement/college savings $ _____

Discretionary spending

Entertainment $ _____

Dining out $ _____

Subscriptions (i.e. streaming) $ _____

Memberships (i.e. gym, activities) $ _____

3. Total up your expenses.

If money will be tight during your transition, lower your spending in whichever categories you can.

THREE

The New Role Selection Process

HAVING HIRED hundreds of salespeople as both a talent development and sales manager, it always comes down to three things that the employer is looking for. It's important to understand what those things are as you start thinking about what *you're* looking for in an employer because it's basically the same idea, but in reverse. Employers want to know:

1. Can you do the job?
2. Will you do the job?
3. Are you the right fit for the organization?

This chapter will take a close-up look at how those three qualifiers break down, and then reverse them as they apply to someone who is in transition and contemplating a new role or job.

Can you do the job?

Simply put, employers want to know if you have the skills, experiences, and level of achievement they're looking for. This can be verified by what hiring managers see on the resume, what they hear on the interview, and the information they get from references. All of that adds up to understanding whether the person has the foundation of skills to do well with a reasonable amount of training.

Reverse Take

As you're looking at a new role and organization, it's important to be honest about whether you meet the minimum qualifications to do the job. If you don't have the proper experience or skills necessary and you somehow still get hired, you'll be starting out at a disadvantage. Even if it's a dream opening, you have to be able to admit if you're not ready for it currently. In that case, at least you'll know which necessary skills you'll need to acquire. You might decide to look for starter positions in that industry or field that can help lead to a similar dream job down the road.

Will you do the job?

This one is a bit more challenging for a hiring manager to predict since it's not as cut and dry as a list of skills. It comes down to whether or not you think a candidate will show up and work hard to reach their goals. More than that, it's making a guess as to whether they will engage fully and stay committed to the new role. It's all about trying to gauge what a person's level of happiness will be.

I've had interviews before in which someone might say that they love outside sales, and thrive on face-to-face client meetings, but the position they were interviewing for was an inside position. At which point, those candidates might say, "That's fine, too," but because they were so passionate about a different kind of job, I found it difficult to believe that they could be equally as happy doing something that's 180 degrees different from their preferred work environment. I usually rejected these types of candidates, not because they weren't qualified, but because I didn't truly believe they would be happy doing the job, and that would eventually lead to them not being fully engaged.

Many times, job seekers try to say what they think the interviewer wants to hear in order to get the job. And those people might squeak through, but they won't be happy once they get started. If you've done this before, I ask you this: What's the point of going through a transition if the end result isn't feeling excitement about the work you're doing?

Reverse Take

If you have the requisite skills to do a job, the next thing you have to think about is if it's something that you can commit to. Remember, once you commit, you're also going to have to endure the learning curve and some of the discomfort we discussed in the last chapter. So, what you need to ask yourself is if the end of the rainbow will be worth it.

It's a tough call sometimes, but you have it in your power to make a reasonable guess. You can do that by asking yourself what it's going to take for you to commit to this new job so that at least in your interview process, you'll have a list of questions to ask. You'll also have an idea of what your deal-breakers are *(see the Worksheet at the end of the chapter)*.

When you get an answer that tells you pretty clearly that the job is not what you're looking for, don't be afraid to thank the interviewer for their time and walk away. There's no shame in that. In fact, from an interviewer's perspective, the second-best outcome is deciding mutually that it isn't going to work out. That way, you shake hands, and everyone can get on with their lives. The worst outcome is hiring someone who isn't right for the job.

Are you the right fit?

Organizations talk more and more about *fit*, and there's a good reason why–people perform their jobs better if they're in an environment in which they feel comfortable. I've conducted interviews in which I've asked candidates what kind of environment they like to work in, and they've given responses that are in total opposition to what their role would entail. For instance, they might say they prefer to work in a quiet workspace so they can focus, or they might thrive in a high-energy environment in which they can feed off their team. Both of those answers are fine, but it's either going to fit the organization's environment or it's not.

Reverse Take

Deciding if you can see yourself as part of a particular organization requires a high level of self-awareness and being very perceptive during your interactions with the company. What vibes do you pick up on during the interview process and as you walk through the office about the kind of organization it is?

Remember the guy who said he loved a quiet workspace? He told me that after he walked through a busy sales floor with loud music playing. He was interviewing for a job in a high team participation company. It was a wonderful and vibrant environment, but not the right one for that prospective hire. I found it odd that the candidate said he'd prefer quiet, so my follow up question was what did you think of our sales floor? He said it was a little loud, but I think I can make it work. For me, I didn't have a huge interest in someone who could make it work. Instead, I anticipated that he would be someone who would be in my office twice a week asking to turn down the music or using the environment as an excuse whenever things didn't go well.

So, readers, ask yourself this: Why would you want to be in an environment that you know going in doesn't suit your style? I get that people need to work and find a job, but if you want to be in a position where you're always looking for a job, then keep picking the wrong ones.

If the writing is on the wall it's not going to be a fit, such as if you hate driving and it's an outside sales job, you need to recognize that this is going to be your life going forward. And you're not doing yourself any favors if you try to make it work. You want to choose an opportunity that gets you fired up and excited.

A Note on Culture

Finding the right fit isn't just about how loud or quiet an office space is–it's about aligning with an organization's culture and values. The problem is it's very tricky to assess a culture in a short amount of time. In order to give you a fighting chance, let's look more closely at what actually comprises a company's culture. Edgar H. Schein wrote a book called *Organizational Culture and Leadership*, and I think he perfectly breaks culture down into three components

1. **Artifacts.** This is anything physical you can see and touch. The office itself, company logos, mission statement and values, and vision statements on the wall are all examples of artifacts. Each item can tell you something. Is it a fun culture or a more serious one? Is the office neat or a mess? Do desks have family photos on them? Do people look proud to be there and full of energy, or like they're just trying to get through the day?

2. **Espoused values.** What does the company say are its most important values? You may see things like we put customer service first, we give 110%, we are a family, we care about the community, etc. For the most part, values will almost always sound great on paper.

3. **Tacit assumptions.** This is the most telling part of culture, but the part that is the most elusive. It's those things that are said around the watercooler. The best scenario is when tacit assumptions match the espoused values. That's difficult to find, but such companies are out there. You need to look for the clues when you walk through the office. If you see someone in the elevator, ask them what they think of their jobs, and if you're making the right move to go work here? Never take one person's

word but ask around and look for a recurring theme. If you get pretty deep in the interview process, you can ask to shadow a rep for a little while to see the job in action. While you're doing that, tap into your inner spy and make sure you're seeing everything and listening. Do you hear one rep bullying another rep? Do you see people getting upset about how leads are dispersed? All these things can add up. What you hear in the interview room might not match the employee experience. You owe it to yourself to make sure you're landing in a spot that's going to fit you.

Your level of motivation will be especially important as you go through your transition—it can help you get up to speed faster, and help you achieve greater results. And if the culture speaks to you, it is more likely that you will feel motivated to do well. At one company I was with, we had a championship belt on the wall of the rep with the highest sales for the month—some interviewees loved the ideas, others thought it was silly. It was just one small way to gauge if our organization was the right culture fit.

Once you establish that you have the skills for the job, that you will commit to doing the job, the last thing to ask yourself is: Is this a place I would want to be at every day, and can I see myself fitting in with these people? If you don't come back with a resounding yes, you might want to keep looking.

Look Inward

Now that you have an idea of the three most important questions to ask yourself as you consider new opportunities, you might be wondering how to make sure that you have all the right answers. Do you really have a good grasp on your skill level? Do you really know what you want in an ideal job? Have you stopped to think about the kind of environment you want to work in?

It's important to assess personal skills and preferences in an honest way when you go through this exercise. Here are some things to think about as you do some self-reflection and self-assessment.

Answer honestly: Can you do the job?

You probably think you have a good sense of your strengths and weaknesses, but sometimes an outside, objective source can be very insightful. Reach out to past supervisors or people who worked with you for an honest assessment of your top skills, as well as the areas in need of improvement. Bear in mind, if you're asking someone from five years ago, you might have updated your skills since then.

But more recent colleagues can help you identify your blind spots. For example, you might be told that you aren't the best when it comes to prospecting clients. If that's something you need to work on and a new job is heavy on prospecting, you might decide it's too high of a learning curve for you to engage in right now. If it's revealed that your top skills are customer engagement, closing, and customer follow-up and you see that a new job requires all of those skills, then you can feel good about checking those boxes.

The key is to talk to people you trust. You might be surprised that something you feel is your strong suit, other people might not; or something you hadn't considered a top skill, others see as your greatest strength.

Think carefully: Will you do the job?

For this question, you have to be honest about your work history, all the way down to the task level. If the job you're looking at requires a lot of phone calls, think back to a period of your career where you had to work the phones. Did you really enjoy that, or was it drudgery to you? Go through each line of the job description, think back to a time when you were doing that task and ask yourself, did that task make me happy?

This is so important because all of the money in the world isn't going to make you enjoy your job if the day-in-day-out tasks feel torturous.

If something in the new job isn't new to you, you can try to make an educated guess by correlating it to other life experiences. For example, if your new role will involve meeting with high level professionals in a face-to-face setting, ask yourself how you feel when you have those kinds of conversations as a client at your accountant's office, or when dealing with a lawyer, or real estate developer. Do you feed off those exchanges? Do you feel out of your league? If you hate being in doctor's offices and you're looking at a job in pharmaceutical sales, be honest with yourself that it might not be the best idea.

When you look at the key tasks of the new job, what emotions do they bring up? Do they excite you? Scare you? Does it sound like the most boring job in the world? Be honest with yourself.

Look closely: Is it a good fit?

As discussed, fit comes down to things like the company culture, the pace, and the workload required. As you look around the office, and as you ask questions, don't dismiss red flags. If you hear people talking about working 60 hours a week and making great money, but you're looking for more work life balance, that might be a nonstarter. If the prospect of making great money sounds exciting for you and you're OK with extra hours, maybe you found the right job.

One more important point is that sometimes you'll feel torn. You might like some aspects of a new opportunity but aren't thrilled about others. At the end of the day, you can't be afraid to try something new. Finding a fit is the hardest part for both the interviewer and the candidate, and it is hard to judge. Sometimes you just have to jump in the water, let your body regulate to that temperature, and then see if it feels comfortable for you.

By taking the time to go through these questions, you'll move forward with far more confidence having gone through this exercise. It might be: "I don't think this is going to work for me, so I'm going to keep looking." Or, "I was nervous about it, but after thinking it through, I realize I have the perfect skills for it, the job duties seem like ones I will enjoy and can commit to, and I already felt like I was part of the family even just during the interview process."

Either way, you'll lower the risk of making the wrong decision.

Looking Forward, Not Back

Going through the three considerations above simply won't work if you come into the process with prejudices, assumptions, and preconceived notions, however. Or put another way, you have to let go of the past in order to move forward toward your future.

Whatever the circumstances were that led you to looking for a new place to work or a change in your career, you need to let go of your previous life in order to give your next opportunity a full shot. To do that, start by understanding two main truths:

You probably won't find the exact same job. If you loved your last job and for whatever reason the company changed or they shut down, and you're looking to find the exact same thing, you're never going to feel satisfied. You'll view every other opportunity as a step in the wrong direction.

What to do: Ask yourself, did you know you were going to love that job when you were in the early stages? Or, did you grow to love it because it gave you skills, and what you needed financially and psychologically to feel good about what you were doing? Usually, positive feelings are built over time. You're never going to find an organization that will give you that same comfortable feeling from the get-go. Also, when you look for sameness, it narrows the field, and in some cases, it might not even exist if your industry has had a drastic change due to regulations, or things moving online. Your best option is to keep an open mind, that way you can recognize which opportunities have the most potential to be as fulfilling–or even better–than your last job.

You probably won't find the total opposite of your last job. If you didn't like your last job, or some situation there left a bad taste in your mouth–maybe you had a management team that wasn't

42

supportive, and it was hard to stay motivated–you might associate every similarity to that job with those negative feelings.

What to do: You have to be a detective here and ask yourself: was a particular aspect of the job really a problem, or did you just hate everything in general because you were so miserable there? I've had prospects come in who were trying to interview me to make sure my opportunity was nothing like the last place they worked. Obviously, there's going to be some commonalities to any situation and if those are met with harsh skepticism from the prospect, chances are I wasn't going to look to bring them aboard.

The bottom line. You can't expect to find the same job you had, but you shouldn't be looking for a job with zero similarities to what you had. Especially if you're in sales, there will also be certain common threads. You need to understand that just because something was executed poorly in your last job doesn't mean it will be in the next one.

If you're not locked into your past (good or bad), you give yourself more of an opportunity to like, enjoy, and prosper in the new career. Of course, all of your experiences that led you to this point are important. But when you look backwards at your very last opportunity, and you're measuring that against your next one, you're allowing your emotional state to dictate a very narrow funnel. You're looking for your new role to fix the feelings or fallout that caused your transition. And it's not up to your next job to do that. You have to look at a new opportunity as something that can grow your career, not as a medicine for the negative feelings that caused your transition.

If your last job closed down, you can't look to your next job to make you feel more secure. If your only concern is about them shutting down, you're going to miss out on asking the right questions. The same is true if you left a job because of a bad management team. If all of your questions are about management support and not about the ins and outs of the actual job, you're missing out on key information.

That's why it's very important to make peace with your last situation and let it go. Yes, you should use your experiences to judge what you're seeing in the new environment, but don't look for the job to fix or replicate what happened in the past. Hanging on to those emotions can lead you to making the wrong choice.

Making the Jump

Say you follow all of the advice above and you consider your skills, if you'll enjoy and engage at the new job, and if the next organization will be a good fit. The good news is that you've given yourself much better odds of finding an opportunity you can feel good about.

However, it's important to understand that even with those tools, you've never going to have *all* of the facts. This process is reducing your risk of walking into a situation that you won't have the skills for, won't have the desire for, or won't be an environmental fit for you. But there are no guarantees.

Once you've done the homework, if you feel reasonably sure at that point, you've got to jump.

You jump with the knowledge that your next job might not be perfect. But I can assure you, if you follow this chapter, you are making a more informed decision on this opportunity than you did for previous roles. You might make a mistake, but you might also stumble into the greatest job you ever had.

On the other hand, it can be very hard to walk away from a job offer when you need a paycheck. But if in your analysis you don't feel like you're going to be happy, you owe it to yourself to hold out for the next opportunity. Remember, with all sales jobs, there's going to be a ramp up time, so if you're going from job to job with an attitude of "I'll give it a shot," you're going to enter a cycle where at the first sign of trouble, you disengage, and you never get to the real money-making part of the job. Your transition will fail, and a few months later, you'll be getting back on the hamster wheel to find the next job.

Some people do that for their entire career.

With that said, you also can't look forever. At a certain point you have to go all in and take a shot if something feels right. At the very least, you should be looking at every opportunity with the lens of "If I take this job and it isn't right, is there still something I can I take away from it?" How will it help me grow? Will it help improve my skill set and make me more viable? If the answer is yes, it makes it easier to move forward because even if it's not the right fit, you're going to get something out of it that's going to benefit your career over the long haul.

TRANSITIONAL TAKEAWAYS

Though you'll never be 100% sure that you're going to be successful as you transition your career, by doing a little bit of work upfront and trusting your gut, you can give yourself the best possible chance.

1. Be open that the new job is not going to fix or replicate the old job. Be open to different ways of doing things and exploring a new career opportunity without trying to shoehorn it into the narrow scope of your last role.
2. Make sure that you're looking at your own skills, desires, and preferences when you look at a new opportunity. Measuring them against each other, instead of just trying to win the job will hopefully keep you from transitioning again in the near future.
3. Look at the new opportunity in a spherical way. Make sure you're clear about the environment in which you'll be doing your job, as well as with whom, and the company's structure.
4. Once you've done the work, you need to trust your gut. If you feel excited about an opportunity, it will help you overcome a lot of obstacles early on. Hopefully it will be a career you have for a long time. But if not, as an escape hatch, at least it can be something that can grow your career in one way or another.
5. Transitioning will be much easier if you can make a reasonable guess that you're going to succeed in the new role.

Motivational Mantra:
"When evaluating a new opportunity, trust yourself... but do the math."

GET-TO-WORK WORKSHEET

Exercise 1: Finding Your Fit

On a scale of 1 to 5 (1 being not at all, 5 being perfect fit) rate your compatibility with the following work environments:

1. Being in the office for the majority of your workday.
2. Primarily contacting your customers by phone.
3. Meeting customers face to face.
4. Spending up to half of your work time in the car on your way to appointments.
5. A quiet work environment where you can concentrate on your work with ease.
6. An exciting environment where the music is playing, and you can feed off the energy of a boisterous office.
7. Working in a team with shared goals, effort and communication.
8. Working individually where you are solely responsible for your work.
9. Executing a long sales cycle with fewer "wins," but a higher value for each win.
10. Executing a shorter sales cycle with a higher volume of "wins" at a lesser value.

Bonus question: Earning the majority of your income through variable compensation (commission).

After completing this sheet, you can use it to evaluate each new opportunity that comes your way. Your 4s and 5s are things that matter most to you; 1s and 2s are things you'll most likely want to avoid; and 3s mean you can go either way. While you might not find a job that matches all of your preferences, if it covers most of the bases, you're in a better position to succeed.

The Transition Begins

Tick, tick, tick. The sight of tracks is giving way to the horizon beyond the theme park. Tick, tick, tick. The track is almost out of view. Time slows down as you creep towards the inevitable plunge. It doesn't matter if you are now second guessing your decision. The tickets have been ripped and the safety bar has been locked down. Tick, tick. You know the next tick you hear will be followed by thunder. It is as inevitable as death, taxes, and for salespeople–objections. You can cry and beg for it to stop, but it won't. You might as well throw your arms up and enjoy the ride. Tick...

FOUR

Getting the Most Out of Training

HAVING DESIGNED foundation training for sales for over a decade and executed hundreds of sales trainings myself, the advice I'm going to give in this chapter is not simply based on my opinion. It's based on hundreds of case studies and having witnessed different approaches to training and finding the common elements that make each one successful.

In this chapter, we're going to discuss the appropriate attitude to bring to training, the preparation you can do for the training before it starts and while you're in the thick of it, strategies for the most common types of training, and more. Let's get started.

Ready Your Mindset

Remember your end goal: To get through your transition as quickly as possible so you can master the job and fulfill your income potential. Having the right attitude as you go into training can help you achieve that goal with fewer bumps in the road.

Even the most experienced and talented salespeople need to approach the training for a new job from a position of curiosity and humility. If you enter into training from the perspective of "I don't know what I don't know," you're starting off on the right foot. You shouldn't treat it like a mystery novel where you're trying to jump ahead of the trainer to figure out the ending. I've had so many trainees say things like, "I know where you're going with that," and that can be very disheartening for a trainer to hear. It has nothing to do with ego—it's because it's a red flag that you could be running into an issue with that trainee. Let me explain.

There are people who put in a massive amount of effort to design this training, and they've probably had some success with it before you got there. There has probably been some trial and error before you walked through the door. So, when you act like you can figure it all out, or that you've learned it all before, it will just end up slowing your progress. I've seen it happen more than a dozen times where someone who should become a great early contributor in their new role didn't end up absorbing the information in their training properly because they assumed they already knew everything. That's the result that literally no one wants.

So instead, take a moment to clear your mind and get ready for training by doing these two key things:

1. **Be curious.** Even if you feel the training you're receiving is basic 101 type stuff, think of it this way. "I may have done something similar to this or had a product close to what we're selling here. But I do not know this sales process, so I need to be open and be curious to absorb as much of this new information as possible." Just because some of it may be familiar, don't let that become a false logic trap where you think you know it all. If you do, you'll end up tuning out all of the other important information and limit your overall experience in the training.
2. **Check your ego at the door.** Arrogance and know-it-all-ism will get in the way of your training. Yes, you have to

have a delusional level of self-confidence to be a great salesperson. Your trainer gets that; they understand your DNA. But you have to reach down deep and find the humility in yourself or you run the risk of squandering your training sessions. There are no extra points for being the smartest guy or gal in the training room. And there's certainly no extra points for attempting to contradict the training before you've received all of it. It's not your purpose to instruct the training class on how you would do it–especially if it's in contrast with what the trainer is saying. It creates confusion and isn't helpful to the rest of the training class. We all want to make a great impression at a new job, but showing everyone you know better in your first couple of days comes off as arrogant. The fact that you found a mistake in the training is not going to get you on the elevator up to the C-Suite. So, bite your tongue if you feel the urge to want to show the room how smart you are and how much you know about sales, because it can become a detriment to you and the training group.

3. **Be a part of the team.** Your main focus in training is learning and building relationships. I've seen training classes that created a lasting bond in which everyone was extremely supportive of each other. But I've also seen overly competitive groups where there ends up being bad blood between new employees who are just starting out– that's counterproductive. Your group is the first team you're going to be on in that organization and you need to value the relationships as much as you can. Training is not the time or place for your competitive nature. It's the time to be supportive of the other people in the group. Everyone is watching. If you alienate your fellow trainees, you put yourself in a hole starting out.

To recap, your mind should be curious, humble, and supportive of the people around you. Truth be told, humility is an uncommon trait for a salesperson, so you may have to work on that one, but you'll be better off if you do. It's sometimes easier for those who are newer because they don't have enough past experiences to develop an ego. However, I've seen veteran, quality salespeople come in and exhibit the appropriate curiousness and humility, and support for their fellow trainees. Not only do they do well, but they end up being someone who is a great value to the organization on just their second or third day. Often, they end up helping some of the newer people who don't have as much experience. Plus, if the experienced sales-person shows that they can be open, it helps validate the training program for everyone else. The sooner the whole training group completely buys into what's going on, the more results they'll see when they exit the training.

Many times, I've been able to trace back a successful training program to one person who came in with the perfect mindset and were vocal about it early on in the group. That helps create a momentum in the group that can ultimately help some people who might not have been as successful out of training otherwise. If you take on the role of humble leader while you're a trainee, you might be someone who will be looked at for leadership opportunities later on.

What to Expect During Training

Once training begins it's like you just hit the top of the rollercoaster and away you go! Time is going to go fast, and you'll be given a lot of information. With the right strategies and an attitude alignment you can get the most out of training. In fact, training can be the most valu-able part of your transition as long as you avoid some of the common mistakes that trainees make.

As we covered, having the attitude that you already know every-thing is going to hold you back. But the flipside of that–being your own worst critic–can be equally as dangerous. In a learning environ-ment, your inner critic is not your friend. While you get through learning mistake-free, that means you're probably not putting forth enough effort. In every training I've done, I expect everyone to make mistakes–and a lot of them! The reason we do tests and exercises is to help bake the information into your knowledge base, it's not to judge you. By being your own worst critic, you're setting unreasonable expectations as a learner. High expectations and standards are a good thing as a general rule, of course, but the idea that you should be an expert during your first attempt at something is not healthy.

If you set the bar too high, here's what happens:

- **You're going to disengage.** You're not going to want to put in the effort because it doesn't feel good when you fail.
- **You'll start to look at that activity as the problem and start to devalue it.** You'll think, "Well, that's stupid anyway. If I thought it was important, I'd be great at it." If you are treating your training as a big waste of time, it will become just that.

As we've discussed, this is the flipside of humility. In this case, it's what allows you to skin your knees while you build skills and knowledge.

Here's an example I've given every training group I've had, and I'm going to share it with you:

Have you ever been around a child who is just learning to walk? It's an exciting moment in a family's life. There are certain clues to show that it's coming. The baby first may start crawling, then lifting up, then cruising (where they take steps with the aid of a coffee table or couch. Once they are standing, everyone in the house is on high alert because you know those first steps are coming any day now.

So, they're cruising, and mom and dad and whomever is coaxing the baby to take a step, and everyone gets excited as the baby lets go and wobbles just a little bit. They take a wobbly step, and everyone starts clapping and is so excited. It's such a beautiful moment to witness. And then the baby, filled with all the joy in the room, takes another step and they're now officially walking. Everybody is overjoyed and clapping, but as the baby goes for the third step, they lose their balance and fall right on their butt. At this moment everyone starts booing, and one uncle even says, "This kid sucks." And the child is left there to feel horrible and learns that if he can't do something right on the first try, that it's a waste of time.

Having read that story, you know that it's all true, up until everyone starts booing. We know that people don't stop clapping. Even when the baby falls, everybody claps because it was amazing progress. That baby also doesn't have an ego. They want to walk. When they fall down, do they feel discouraged? No way. They get back up and do it again. And again. They don't even think about it. They don't look at those failed attempts as black marks on their ego. Barring physical limitations, the success rate of children who try to walk is 100%. Everybody figures it out eventually, most times with a lot of falling down in the process. But it's because the child is open, and there's no pressure for immediate success, all they do is keep their eyes on the prize. They always get there.

So why don't we have the same 100% success rate as we try to learn new things as we get older? Because we develop an ego and identity and create expectations that are unrealistic or unreasonable. This is also what keeps talented people from trying new things. As you're training you have to understand that you're never going to get great at a new skill if you beat yourself up when it doesn't go well. You have to change your relationship with failure during a learning period in your life.

In fact, you should be excited to fail, to progress, to go fast, to take chances. If the exercise is a mock sales presentation, don't be worried how you look or how smooth your approach is or that you get every single thing right–be willing to make mistakes in service to your objective. You'll definitely become an expert much faster with that approach. Take away a lesson from the wreckage and apply it to how you're going to perform next time. If you can do that without letting it take an emotional toll, you've put yourself in the class of learner who will be able to cut down their learning curve and be able to reduce their transition time. You'll also have less discomfort because your whole identity isn't wrapped up in you being better than you should be at a time when you don't know everything. The reason you're in training isn't for you to ace everything.

Instead, be the baby. Stumble and laugh your way through it. Hopefully the training is creating an environment that's a safe place to fall down. But even if it's not, care a little bit less about what everyone else thinks. There's no reason to limit the efficacy of your training because you're afraid or embarrassed or you're your own worst critic. During your training, try to have the same level of encouragement for yourself as you would for that baby who's learning to walk.

Preparation Before Training

One thing that has always baffled me is how little prep people do prior to training. That's because it's really so simple to get a leg up by doing a few simple things. Preparation will help you avoid feeling so overwhelmed at all of the information that's going to be coming at you.

Plus, you'll gain valuable context about the company and industry, so you'll absorb the information more easily. That all means that you'll feel more confident, making for a smoother training and transition. Here are some things you should do:

1. **Explore the company website.** It sounds simple, but you'd be surprised by how many people don't take advantage of the treasure trove of information that is housed on their new company's website. If I had to guess, I'd say 80% of trainees don't inspect them thoroughly. Yet, company websites market their products, talk about mission and values, link to advertising and marketing materials. You can put yourself at a huge advantage by reading every word on the website. Make notes. Make sure you understand what the value proposition is for the customer, and what the features and benefits are of the

products and services. You're not going to understand everything and that's OK. Write questions down, wait until you hear it in training, and then ask if it hasn't been answered already. If the company has a staff page, take it a step further and check out LinkedIn to see where people worked before. Be a detective. You might pick up some hints as to what this company considers important, and that can help you align your mentality for that job. Ultimately, if you can go into training with a solid idea of what they sell, how they sell it, and what the marketing tries to push in order to get a customer excited about their product, you're a step ahead. Take it all in. Do just that and you'll put yourself in the top 20% of the training group.

2. **Stalk the company on social media.** Once you land a job, you should immediately begin following and checking the company's social media profiles on a daily basis. Just the type of social media they choose to prioritize can clue you in about the audience they are trying to engage. Does the social media have personality? If so, you can get a sense of the company's voice. If they're playful, you might know you can be a little more playful with interactions with customers. These are all clues that can help you begin your training with a clear understanding of the company's goals, what it's trying to achieve, and how you fit into that.

3. **Check out the competition.** Being in the top 20% of the class is great, but if you want to make it to the top 2%, you'll take your homework a step further and look at competitor companies. These are the organizations that will be competing for the same customers as you. Those companies also have websites and social media, so go ahead and do the same exercise as above so you can compare your company to the competition. Each one is bringing some value to the table, so it's better to know what you're up against and where potential weaknesses are so you can begin to work within those confines and

put together your strategy. Once you start selling, you'll come up against questions about this offer or that company and doing this research will put you in a good position. The pitfall you want to avoid while you're doing this is falling in love with another company's offering. I once had a trainee tell me that our company couldn't compete with X company because they offered something we didn't. Not only was that notion far from true, but that person still didn't fully understand what our company was all about. While you're in training, you don't really know the whole back story. Perhaps they found they don't want to target a particular type of customer, so they don't offer a certain feature–if so, that was likely a tactical decision. Here's an example I like to give: Denny's menu has 150 things on it, while another restaurant might only have 10 items. Does that mean they can't compete with Denny's because they don't offer a "Moons Over My Hammy" sandwich? The point is, you only know the customer-facing marketing at this stage. Until you learn about the inner workings of the company, you won't fully understand the strategy.

4. **Get industry educated.** Once you've looked at the customer-facing vehicles of your company and its competitors, you can do some industry research. Industry periodicals will assume a certain level of knowledge so you might not understand the lingo just yet. Don't worry– you don't need to get too far down in the weeds here, but it can't hurt to subscribe to whatever industry publications are available online or in print. This isn't for you to be an expert before your first day of training. It's just to begin familiarizing yourself with the industry you're going to be working in before training.

5. **Optional: Listen to the sales pitch.** If you really want to do some sleuthing, fill out an online form on the company website to create a lead so you can get someone on the

phone and hear the sales pitch. Most companies won't necessarily share this advice with you, but don't feel too bad about it. You can find out after the fact which salesman called you and buy them a coffee. Of course, if you have a friend in the organization, you might just ask them to set up a mock presentation/pitch for you. Either way, it's a neat little trick to come in even more prepared. Even if you end up with someone who's not their best on that call, it's a great tool prior to training. If you don't feel OK about it, don't do it. It's not going to make or break your career, but it's just another cool reference point for you as you see the training unfold.

By spending time on the research above, you won't walk into your training blind, and will be all the more comfortable as you proceed.

Daily Prep During Training

While you can give yourself an advantage by doing the things discussed in the last section, once the training begins, it's even more vital that you do some daily homework. You're going to be getting internal company information that is designed to prepare you to be successful selling. Some training days are heavy on information, while others focus on exercises that are more interactive. You might also watch some video content. And almost all training has some sort of manual. Here's what you should do each day of training to help yourself process it all.

1. **Take notes throughout the day.** Even during exercises, right down things that jump out as important. If someone asks a question that you don't know, jot it down with the answer. Don't assume something is going to stick, or that you'll remember it a month from now. During breaks, flesh out your notes while the information is still fresh in your mind. A lot of studies that show you only retain a

quarter of what you hear after a few days. But if you hear something, write it down, and read it back, that retention is much greater. And if you take it even further, once you execute the techniques that you've written down and then teach it to someone else, that's when you've gone the full circle of training and mastering a skill. At that point, the chances of your training being a success will go through the roof.

2. **Review your notes.** After training, take a couple of hours to decompress. After your brain has had a little time to bounce back but before you go to bed, go back over the day's notes. Organize your thoughts as to what you were trained on that day. Then, spend another half hour the next morning before training looking over the notes one last time. That gives you a full hour of recap that you can build upon the next day.

Keep in mind, your trainer technically can't tell you that you need to study on your own time, because it would be asking you to do work that the company is not paying you for. With that said, understand this is on you. You can do extra work or go over your notes all you want, even if your trainer doesn't recommend it. It's something that you should do.

How to Be Physically Ready for Training

You may find yourself at the point in your career when you can get up, hop in the shower, make it to your first meeting, and ace it. Training is not that time. Sleep is important for a learning mind. So if you're already getting up early to go over your notes, that means you should consider a self-imposed curfew. A 10 p.m. bedtime while you're on your training will give you a major advantage because you're going to show up bright-eyed and bushy-tailed. You'll be clear-minded, your attention span will be longer.

If your favorite band is in town and you want to go out for a late-night concert during your first week of training, I would have to question how bad you want to succeed in this new job. How short do you want your transition to be? There are not many things more important than how you earn your living, so some sacrifices might need to happen. You can still do things, just do it early. If your birthday or anniversary happens to fall during training, do a lighter version of what you would have done. What better gift to give yourself than to exhibit a little discipline and make your training week go smoother? Whenever I see someone in training that looks like they were out the night before, my immediate thought is that this is a person who is not taking this as seriously as they should. Their chance of success is lower than it would have been if they were a little more respectful of their body and time.

Get to bed early so you can show up having just reviewed your notes from the day before. Have your coffee in hand and be ready to go. You'll perform your best if you're rested and prepared, and you'll improve your chances of getting positive results.

Different Types of Training - What to Expect

Now you're prepared, your mentality is set, and it's time to jump in and talk about the different kinds of training you might encounter. While there are a lot of different ways companies choose to engage trainees, I will cover some of the most common ones and provide some tips on how to approach each one.

The standard classroom training

This is like your typical high school or college class set up where you're seated at a table with your book or computer and somebody is teaching the training. They may be working from a PowerPoint deck or white board. They're giving you the information and asking some questions along the way. This should be a very familiar feel. It's the way we've learned in our lives, and it's pretty standard for you to experience this at some point in the training.

So how can you navigate the training classroom, even if you weren't the best student the first time around (raises hand!)?

1. **Pay attention.** It sounds almost too basic, but you'd be surprised at how many trainees I've seen check out. Your focus is very important here. You really have to be plugged in and really listen. Keep your eyes wide. If you hear something you don't understand, jot it down to ask later. Take lots of clear notes that you will understand even a year from now if you pulled them out. It's absurd to think you can hear eight hours of information and remember it all. It's OK to ask the trainer to repeat something or even slow down. They won't mind if you ask, trust me.

2. **Don't be afraid to ask questions, and don't worry about how you'll look.** As a trainer I can tell you for sure, I haven't always been perfectly clear. Almost always, when someone asks a question, there is someone else in the room who has that same question. It gives the trainer the opportunity to take you to the next level of understanding.

3. **Answer questions.** There's nothing worse than having 10 people in a class and none of them speak up when you try to engage them or get them to participate. When trainers ask questions, they're trying to create a more interactive experience for the entire group.

They're not trying to catch you if you don't know an answer. Go ahead and raise your hand so you can contribute something to the topic being covered.

Video training

This type of training involves sitting at a computer watching a video of someone training you. A lot of companies will mix this with other types of training. A lot of times for compliance reasons, some portions of training will be given this way, so the company is certain that the message gets across exactly as they want.

So how can you get through what could potentially be a *boring* part of training and make the most of it?

The key strategy is to pay attention. Even though no one is watching you, I'd still recommend staying in the habit of being the best learner you can be. Take notes and jot down questions in the same way you would with a live trainer.

Mock sales training

With this portion of training, you get to start practicing your pitch with your group. Many times, training programs use a triad system: One person is the salesperson, one is the customer, and one is the observer. I've found it to be one of the more valuable training tools. You're going to see variations of this throughout sales training. Some might be done over the phone; other times you might have to walk into an office if you're simulating an outside sales job.

No matter the format, here's how to make the most of mock sales exercises:

- *If you're the salesperson:* You might have an overwhelming tendency to overdo it early on in training. By that I mean you're tempted to try to build this amazing rapport with the fictional client to show everyone what a silver-tongued savant you are. But that's far less important than following the process. Don't feel the need to have a big showy sales call. It's more useful to execute on whatever the purpose of the mock presentation is. If it's that you just learned about the sales process, you should be checking off all those boxes. Don't be afraid to make a mistake, but don't abandon the process by falling back on strategies you've used in the past. If you're not sure what to do going into it, ask some questions. Just remember that this isn't your time to shine just yet. It's more about getting comfortable with a process or a product line to build some muscle memory, rather than freewheeling it on charisma alone.

- *If you're the customer:* Chances are there is going to be some sort of needs development in the mock presentation. Make sure your needs for the product are in alignment with what you're telling the salesperson. Think it through and take a moment to think about how difficult of a customer you want to be. There's not a whole lot to gain from busting chops and being the worst customer ever. That's not helping anyone, and it becomes a waste of time since it's not appropriate for this level of training. But you don't want to be a total cupcake of a customer who gives up immediately without much probing either. The best approach is to have an ounce of skepticism like a normal customer would. Don't make the sale easy but make it attainable. Prior to the exercise, get in alignment with your group. Ask each other how tough the *customer* role should be? Maybe the *salesperson* wants you to throw a curveball or two. Throughout training, if you do a lot of mock presentations, try varying your approach as well so it's always like they're pitching a different customer.

- *If you're the observer:* This role is important since you don't have the burden of going through the presentation so you can focus on the interaction. Your job is to offer the best notes because you are fully in tune to what's happening. Don't zone out. Don't start thinking, "This is or isn't what I would do." Don't let your preconceived notions get in the way. Be more like a news reporter who records the facts, and then editorialize just a little bit. You can say something like, "I noticed the call stalled there. Maybe you could have done XYZ." You can still add your opinion, but don't measure their performance against your style. Another thing you don't want to do is tell everyone how great they are. Yes, you're trying to be supportive and a great teammate, but if you're only giving good news during an exercise like this, they won't get much value out of it. If you really want to be supportive and a good friend, point out the good, the bad, and the ugly. Prior to starting this exercise, ask your partners about the level of honesty they are comfortable with. This can help illustrate that your criticism is coming from a place of wanting to help. Find the right balance between being honest and not being overly critical. Focus on the most important things they need to work on without getting nitpicky.

Shadowing

Because of the nature of sales, there are a lot of opportunities to see how to do the job the right way. Shadowing in sales is very common practice. For outside sales, you might get in the car with a sales manager; if it's inside, you will plug in a headset and listen in on a call. It gives you the chance to watch an expert prior to your trying it. How to get the most out of shadowing:

1. **Pay attention to everything that's happening.** It's not just about the sale itself. It's also how the salesperson executes all of the processes that go along with getting the sales. It's a chance to learn about workflow so that you can get comfortable in your position sooner. A lot of sales trainees do not take full advantage of shadowing. They listen in, but they miss out on what the person is doing digitally or paperwork wise.
2. **Take notes.** That is key for all types of training, as you can see. If you hear something that's different than what you heard in training, write it down. Ask the sales rep about it later or ask your trainer about it. Make sure you're clear on how to execute the process.
3. **Ask questions.** If you're sitting with somebody for hours at a time, you might feel the urge to want to treat it like you're hanging out. It's certainly OK to ask about the

snacks in the break room or the place in general but try to keep at least 80% of your questions on the sales process, the product line, the overall presentation, and the customer interaction. Those are the things you want to be clear on.

4. **Show appreciation.** When it's over, if you just get up and leave and don't show any appreciation, that person will probably not go out of their way to look out for you. On the other hand, if you play your cards right, you might end up with someone who can act as a mentor. Remember, this is someone that the company has identified as being someone you should emulate, so it's someone you want to be in with down the line.

Quizzes and tests

I'm a big fan of having periodic checks on the group to make sure everyone is on the same playing field, and to make sure I'm doing my job as a trainer. But I've had many reactions to such testing. Some people aren't great test takers. That's OK. Just know that for the most part, trainers are not looking for perfection, or to even grade you. They just want to make sure that you're coming along and you're getting it.

A lot of companies will have certification testing for which you will have to achieve a minimum score in order to move on. But even in those cases, there is usually a chance to retake the test if you didn't pass, so don't stress it too much.

Here's a little secret: The company spent a lot of money to recruit you and bring in the door, so they're not looking to give you up that easily. If you blow a test, it's not the end of the world. If there's something you aren't getting, you'll learn it. Take testing seriously and with the intention of doing as well as you can. But, the result itself is more about seeing where you are proficiency-wise. If there is something that you're struggling with, don't' be afraid to ask about it. Tests are just another learning tool to help you get where you're going. By testing your knowledge, it's another way of cementing information in your mind and making it easier to recall later on when you need it.

How Setting Can Affect Your Training

Companies choose a wide array of training settings, but it breaks down into two big categories: on-site training and off-site training. A lot of bigger companies that have multiple offices throughout the country find it more efficient to do foundation training in one location, and they fly in people from different regions. Whereas some organizations are smaller, or they have such varied local offerings so they may keep training internal and on-site. Each one has its own advantages, but ultimately, it's up to you to make the most of your time.

Advantages of off-site training

Off-site training gives you the chance to really immerse yourself in the training process. Training is the star of the show rather than the extra thing happening in the middle of a regular business day. While most people have the emotional intelligence to understand the importance of foundation training, when you're on-site, you might encounter an attitude from some workers who feel like you're in their way. But if you're off-site, you don't have to experience that.

Off-site training also takes you out of your home and sometimes away from your hometown, so you won't have to worry about your personal routine. That could potentially give you a better chance to review your training information and get to bed early. You won't have to pick anyone up from soccer practice. You can focus on just being a learner in a place where you can just be a learner. That's a wonderful advantage. Don't look at it as this is going to be awful being at a hotel for two weeks. Take advantage of how great it can be to have access to that level of immersion that will help you prepare to crush it in your career.

Finally, there's a social advantage to off-site training in that it puts you with people who are in the same boat as you. I've seen this go wrong, too, where people turn it into something akin to pledge week. But as long as you have self-control, it will provide the chance to start building your support network. This is especially true when there are people coming from a lot of different places because you're building friends throughout the organization. Remember that example from Chapter One about Maggie who created a study group during her training? That group created a bond and they had a support system in place the day they started.

As for downsides for off-site training, there is really only one. It's that you're learning everything in a vacuum away from the business, so you won't be seeing the lessons in action until you actually start the job.

If you take advantage of the opportunity to build a support system, the extra focus, and the immersion into the information, you can come away from training feeling ready to start your job, and hopefully with some new friends.

Advantage of on-site training

The biggest perk of training in the same place that you'll be working is that you're going to see everything happening right before you as you're learning. You'll get to experience the inner workings of the company. And, it's a more centralized opportunity to build relationships. If you were off-site, you'd be primarily dealing with the talent development team. But on-site, you can build your network within the organization because interactions can happen anywhere, from the elevator to the break room.

The other major perk is that your regular life can go on fairly uninterrupted. You still get to be in the comfort of your home, see your family, and sleep in your bed. Depending on your personality, this can be a plus or a minus, but many people will be glad that they don't have to disrupt their entire routine.

Finally, you'll get a taste of what it's like going to and from work so you can figure out your best route and start developing a routine. As far as your transition process goes, onsite training puts you one step closer to getting used to your new job.

No matter which type of training you are given, know that both types are valuable and can be successful for you. Stick to your training goals of absorbing all of the pertinent information and building relationships and you'll complete your training successfully.

TRANSITIONAL TAKEAWAYS

We covered a lot in this chapter: the right mindset to have during training, the preparation to do before and during training, and the kinds of training you will encounter. The biggest lessons you should come away with are:

- **You need to be accountable for the results of your own training.** Your attitude, effort, and preparation while in training are completely up to you. No one can set that for you. The training can still happen but the only thing that is going to impact your attitude, effort, and preparation is you. Own the learning process. It's on you to learn. Everybody learns differently but it's your responsibility to make sure you get everything you need from the training. "They didn't teach me enough," is not an appropriate excuse once you're on the job.
- **Love yourself through the process.** Don't be your own worst critic. If you can allow yourself to fail and fail often, you're going to learn a lot more than if you're afraid to make a mistake or look bad. And when you do make a mistake, shake it off.

Motivational Mantra:
"Check your ego at the door and get ready to work: It's training day."

GET-TO-WORK WORKSHEET

Exercise 1: Training Accountability Checklist

Aim to check off all or most of these boxes the next time you go through a sales training program.

- ❏ Research the company website thoroughly.
- ❏ Follow company on social media.
- ❏ Explore competitor websites and social pages.
- ❏ Read industry blogs and periodicals.
- ❏ Allow training the chance to teach you something new.
- ❏ Contribute to class discussions; but don't be a showoff.
- ❏ Pay attention, take notes, and stay engaged.
- ❏ Review material for a half hour at the end of the day, and a half hour the next morning.
- ❏ Get adequate sleep.
- ❏ Be friendly and supportive of fellow trainees. Show
- ❏ appreciation to sales pros that you shadow.

FIVE

Transitioning to the Sales Arena

BEFORE JUMPING into the sales arena on your first day, it's important to take a moment to take stock of what you've accomplished thus far. You've gotten through the first major phase of your transition and are ready to begin the real work.

As we said earlier, transitions are hard, but they can also be quite rewarding, and you can make the most of those rewards by simply acknowledging that they have happened because you have navigated certain parts of the transition that could be very tricky.

Here's what you've accomplished so far:

- **You've figured out why you're making your transition.** For some of you, that's an easy answer–if it was thrust upon you or if your life has changed in some way. For others, you might have had the opportunity to figure out exactly what you were looking for so you could increase your chances of finding it.
- **You've looked at organizations and selected your job.** You've done the homework to make sure that it's going to be a good fit for you, and that you'll be able to spend a long time at that organization. That's not to be taken

lightly. I'm sure if you're like me, you have a lot of examples of times when you took a job because you needed a job, and you didn't put much thought into whether or not that job was going to be good for you. But this time around you did the homework, and you should have a bit more confidence because you did do the work.

- **You aced your training.** What could have caused a lot of anxiety, you were able to successfully get through by prioritizing your actions and making sure you were prepared each day. You've developed a proper attitude, and hopefully you've already begun to build long lasting relationships in that organization.

Getting through all of these steps is a testament to your commitment to the transition, and your approach. So, before you get cracking, let's celebrate a little bit. If it's your last Friday of training and you start on Monday, do something nice for yourself. Do something just solely for the enjoyment of it, whether it's spending time with friends or family, or if it's a small splurge doing something you love. Because now you're getting to the fun part of the job. It will still have challenges, but right now, it's a good time to rejoice about the fact that you're almost through your transition. A lot of hard work is up ahead but you're prepared for it and that's certainly something to celebrate. So cheers to you!

From Training to the Sales Floor

Now that you've had your moment to celebrate, it's time to move forward with some practical strategies for how you can enter the next phase of your transition and keep the momentum going. That is, taking what you've learned in training and stepping onto the sales floor.

But before we get into the strategies, I wanted to share a few thoughts about first impressions. To do that, I'm going to make an unexpected correlation between stand-up comedy and your first days in a new sales job.

With over 20 years of stand-up comedy experience, I've taken the stage more than 1,000 times. And each of them was an opportunity to make a first impression. As you're completing your training, I discovered an interesting parallel between stand-up comedy and starting a new sales job.

In my early career, I'd walk on stage and my initial focus was always to please the crowd. I would worry: How are they going to respond to me? Later on, I realized that it was a very self-focused way of thinking. I missed out on a lot by thinking I was stepping out there to be judged, rather than thinking that the audience and myself were part of the same organism the moment I stepped on the stage.

As I progressed, my focus started to change. I started to go on stage and take a moment to breathe the room in, to get a feel for what my audience was like, and start the set with more of a focus toward being a part of that organism, rather than being something separate from it that's being judged.

The first impression happens a lot faster in the stand-up world than it does starting a new job, but there are a lot of similarities. When you go in as the outsider hoping to be liked, hoping to be successful, and wanting to assert yourself as a top performer, you can miss out on building a support system within that organization. You may even rub people–the ones who have the potential to become your mentors–the wrong way. If you are new to an industry, product, or process, the people with more experience can offer insights that can be game-changing for you. So rather than worry if people are going to like you or try to impress others, be much more focused on what you're bringing to the table. That's a much more productive way to start off.

Just like with comedy, you can walk into your new office and get a chilly response. You can respond by panicking and taking it out on the crowd, or you can stay the course and allow the audience to warm up to you. You don't know what kind of reception you're walking into. Depending on what time of the month you're starting, other salespeople might be too focused on their individual or team goals to give you the time of day. There are all sorts of things that may have happened just before you hit the floor. The seat you're in could be the former spot of the favorite salesperson who just left. That's not your fault at all, but it could still affect the reaction you get if people expect you to fill those shoes. It's kind of like having to go on stage after an awesome performance.

But instead of worrying about all of that, try coming into the organization and owning your place in it. What that means is you now have a responsibility to be a defender and a facilitator of the culture that's there. And you can start by building your support structure within the organization.

So, take my advice as both a comedian and a seasoned sales profession: make sure you're stepping onto the big stage focused not on your selfish needs for approval, but instead of what you can do to fit in. With the right approach, people will want to root for you and gravitate toward you in the early stages of your career, and that can go a long way.

Thanks for indulging me in that analogy. Now let's get into the three biggest things you can do to ensure this next phase of your transition goes smoothly–and, as a result, wind up with adoring fans in your new workplace.

1. Study and check yourself.

Imagine you took a college course and then after the first two weeks, you stopped studying. How do you think you would do on the final exam? I would guess not great. So, when you exit training with the idea that you have everything you need to be successful long term, that's insane. Companies don't have the luxury to train you for six months. So, while the formal training period is over, the learning must continue if you're going to reach your full potential in your new positions.

We've talked extensively about taking great notes and making sure you're studying in the evening and the morning. There's no reason for that not to continue as you go through your first few months in the position. The only difference is now you have real-world experiences that you can start to measure against your training. Plus, you have a sales manager, or maybe a team lead and a sales manager, who can help guide you in your studies as you move forward.

Everything you do in between the time you punch in and punch out should be part of an educational autopsy that you conduct later that evening and the next morning. Is there something in the work-flow that's just not clicking for you? Is there a little piece of the process that didn't stick, or that you didn't fully understand? Rather than get woefully behind, like I've seen happen hundreds of times, make a commitment to examine and refine your process as you go. Sometimes these autopsy sessions will be fun because you'll see a little early success. But even when you make a sale, you might have some things that can be improved and some areas that will require a little bit of study. Don't be hard on yourself but be critical of what's happening in relation to the sales process that the org wants you to use.

In many cases, there will be some sort of a training follow-up mechanism with talent development or your manager where you'll have a weekly coaching interaction. If that isn't offered, ask for it. Have a set time to go over what you've experienced in a given week, to go over your notes, and to get feedback on what you've been doing. Don't be afraid to share with them a time where a sales interaction went bad because that's how you will learn the most. Just as important as including your support team, you also have to put the study time in on your own. If you do this for 90 days, your chances of succeeding in your new role will go up exponentially.

If you don't, you could potentially stray off course. While I don't think anyone's sales process is the only right way to do it, if your organization uses one process that everyone is measured by, it allows team leads to give consistent help and mentoring. If you're off doing your own thing and there's no process being employed, it's tough for you to get help when you need it. That's why I tell new hires that while this might not be the only or best way to do this, this is the way you need to master before we're interested in hearing about your way of doing it. Once you've had success, then you can talk to your manager about getting a little creative.

For the purposes of this book, creativity in your sales process is not something you're going to do. Now is the time to learn the process being prescribed by the organization so you can master it. From there, depending on management flexibility you can take some liberties at that point. Think of it this way: If you want to be the best improvisational jazz musician, then you first need to know the song better than anybody else. So make sure you know your sales process inside and out before you start tinkering with it.

That goes back to studying, not just from your training book, but from your sales interactions. If your manager can get you your sales calls to listen to on your off hours, get them. That's gold! Listening to yourself can be cringeworthy at times, but you need to start measuring your interactions by the standards set in training. By taking 30 minutes an evening and 30 minutes in the morning to do that, you're going to cement all of the things you learned in training and apply them to your real-world job.

For those who exit training and never pick up their manual again, it's quite likely that they will slowly corkscrew away from the training. It's going to happen in sales more than with any other profession because we get pushback from customers and it doesn't feel good. Here are some things I've heard happen on the countless calls from new reps I've listened in on:

- You might not develop the customer needs because that can be uncomfortable, so now you have a client but no idea why they are speaking with you.
- You're not asking for money because you haven't done the work to deserve the sale at that point. You might state a price, but you're not asking for the business.
- When the customer objects to end the conversation, you don't respond to that objection and redirect it to a sale.

How successful do you think these approaches will be? Not very, but these are actually fairly common mistakes and the reason is usually because the salesperson is not listening to themselves regularly and has no idea how far they've wandered from the path.

When I've played calls like that for sales reps, they are equally astonished because they didn't realize they weren't doing the fundamental things to earn a sale. To avoid going down that path, study your sales interactions, and challenge yourself *(use the checklist worksheet at the end of the chapter to help)*.

If you're shying away because you had a bad interaction, that's only going to lead to a lot more bad interactions, so hold yourself accountable.

2. Strive to be the best at something.

Salespeople are very competitive by nature, so it makes sense that you always want to be the best in the room. It's definitely part of my DNA, and I think if you're reading this

book, you are probably the same. But here's the thing–it's very hard to be the best salesperson when you're just starting out on day one. So, what can you do? You just have to redirect your efforts so that you're focused on just a couple of key areas for which you *can* be the best starting on day one.

- **You can be the hardest worker in the room.** This requires discipline, effort, and pride in doing your job well. Within your first week, everyone may notice that you are really working hard. You can even start to put challenges on other people who'll see how motivated you are. This is not about becoming popular or feeding your ego–it's about allowing people to see who you are and what you're about, so they begin to trust you and want to help.
- **You can become a product expert.** If you were to quiz most salespeople about the minutia of the product they're selling, most aren't going to fare too well. Although

product knowledge does not necessarily equate sales success, it is something that can help you develop early sales confidence as you transition into the gig. By becoming a product expert early on, you could potentially know the most about the product in the entire office. It just requires daily attention. I worked in a company that sold 6 or 7 insurance products with super long contracts, but they never changed. So each day, I took one contract and just read through it and kept doing that until I knew everything that was in each of them. Again, product knowledge does not guarantee sales success, and inundating your customer with product details probably isn't going to help move the needle. But product knowledge will help you to pair the right product to each customer. Once you develop their needs, you can make sure you're putting them in the right product, and that's a wonderful thing early on that can result in strong customer retention.

When you focus on these two behaviors and the confidence that goes along with them, it can carry over into other aspects of the job. We've talked about discomfort earlier in the book, and when you first start talking to customers with money on the line, you'll really feel it. If you stumble through your process, it can be really deflating. Striving to be the best by working hard and studying the product can carry you through the rough spots. Some days you're going to feel exhausted because learning something new can be tiring. But if you can push yourself through with your effort, not only will you be the hardest working person in the room, but you'll eventually achieve a higher degree of success than you would have otherwise.

3. Seek mentorship.

In an ideal world, your sales manager will be helpful and have plenty of time for you, but that's not always the case. Sometimes they're tasked with a lot, or they're job is more of being a statistician than a coach. Should you be faced with that, start asking around–who do you think the best salesperson here is? Who do you think has the best attitude for success at this job? If you ask those questions to everybody you encounter, you're going to start hearing the same names popping up, and those are the people you need to be around.

Salespeople like to have their egos stroked, so if you're nervous that they won't be willing to help you, all you need to do is say, "I've been asking everybody who the best salesperson is in the office and most of them say it's you. I want to be really good at this job and would love the opportunity to talk to you about what I'm doing and get your thoughts. Maybe I can listen in on some of your sales inter-actions and have you critique mine if and when you have time." Chances are the person you ask will be so flattered that they'll be amped up to help you.

There is one caveat–just because someone is the best at some-thing doesn't mean they're the best at explaining it. If you have a team leader or manager, they can help you filter the advice you get until you have enough understanding to filter it yourself. Otherwise, you'll sometimes get conflicting advice and won't know what to do. I'll give you an example: I live in Los Angeles for years now, and I still don't know what to do in an earthquake because I've only heard two pieces of advice: 1. Stand in a doorway, and 2. Don't stand in a doorway.

Should you get conflicting advice from a couple of top salespeo-ple, don't be afraid to go back and say, "I've been thinking about your advice, but it seems to be in conflict with this other thing I'm hearing. What are your thoughts?" By being the hard working one who takes the initiative to ask questions like that, people are going to want to help you. They'll be impressed that you're seeking help right out of the gate and will be thrilled to mentor you. The best part is that this is something you can do right away regardless of your talent level that will help you work toward completing a very successful transition.

Meet Michelle, the Breakout Sales Success

Michelle was a new hire in a training class of five people with a great attitude, but the scouting report on her was that although she'd be a great culture fit, she might not be a high performer. Coming out of training, Michelle worked tirelessly and really stood out amongst all of the sales team. Almost immediately, she started really leaning on the top performers in the office and got their expert advice along the way. After about a month of Michelle coming in with a wonderful attitude and really putting her back into each and every day, performance-wise, she was still average.

But she was great to be around, was a positive contributor, and good for the culture and that was a win. She wasn't getting any harsh feedback, but during those first few months, her results were good–not great. Her work ethic was off the charts, and she had a solid network of mentors who wanted to help her. Her positivity and attitude caught fire, and everyone loved spending time with her. In addition to her regular weekly sales coaching sessions, in her off-time she was meeting up and talking sales with people. We noticed somewhere around her second month that she began answering others' questions about products and processes. It was evident that she wanted to be the best at something.

In month three, she ran into a slump that is all too common. It was rough, but she salvaged it at the end through determination.

By month four, though, something really special started to happen. Out of 80+ salespeople, Michelle broke into the top 10. Now, technically, month four goes beyond the scope of this book, but it's important that I make an exception so you can hear the rest of Michelle's story. By month six, Michelle was in the top five. I can't stress enough that no one ever saw this coming. Nobody predicted this kind of success for Michelle because, frankly, she wasn't the most skilled salesperson. She was average in every discernible way with the exception of her attitude, her effort, and her desire. And lo and behold–that average talent ended up with extraordinary results.

Now, it didn't happen right away, which is why we took a look past her first 90 days. But what was unique about Michelle is that she actually did many of the things we recommend in the book, and she ended up being a breakaway success story. From a talent to success ratio standpoint, there was no better.

I remember one day she walked by my office and waved as she went by as she always did. I called her in to see how she was taking to the job. She said she felt like she was still catching up, but she loved the culture and wanted to do well and be a part of it. "I want to contribute to this culture, and I know the only way to do that is get sales," she said. It was such a simple and honest interpretation of her situation and I was Michelle's number one fan from that moment on. What a great attitude! She didn't say I want people to like me; she said I want to contribute.

Rather than wait to see what would happen, this is somebody who came in and said I see what you're doing, and now I'm going to do it. That is music to any leader's ears. It's worked out for Michelle the most. To this day, she makes great money and is beloved by her colleagues, and all it took was curiosity, positivity, effort, and desire. And now that Michelle is established in her job, guess who the first person is to engage with new hires and to offer to spend time with them? Yep, you guessed right.

Applying what Michelle did to your transition takes a lot of effort. But the great thing about sales is you get paid for your effort–you make more money. That's the beautiful thing about this job. Your hard work will not just get you through the transition period, but it can put you on your way to breakaway success.

Michelle was probably the best example I've ever seen of someone maximizing their talent and minimizing their learning curve. I wish I would have done any transition in my life as well as the woman who we all thought for sure would only be an average performer at best.

Meet Alan, the Failed "Best Salesperson in the Room"

Alan was a high-performing salesperson who had a tremendous series of interviews before joining the company. He began his training and almost immediately created a little concern because he was not seemingly engaged. When the talent development manager raised this concern, Alan leaned in and said, "I've been doing this for a long time and I'm just trying to get through training so I can make money but trust me–you don't have to worry about me."

When it came time for testing, he did well enough, and he began his first day of work. The first thing he did was alert everyone that he was really experienced and really good at sales and he was going to do things no one had ever seen before. And whatever the sales records were didn't matter because he was going to destroy them. He was a little arrogant (to say the least), but not a bad guy. We had a culture that valued mentorship and helping each other so despite his cockiness, people were trying to assist him. His team leads, his manager, and other helpful people reached out, but at each turn, he wasn't receptive. He continued to say, "Trust me, the results will be there."

In his first month, it seemed everything he said was accurate. He didn't break records, but he was the highest performer of the training group. Because of that, Alan's manager gave him more leeway than he should have, so instead of coaching sessions, it became more of a check-in.

Month two started off great, landing him in the top salesperson position for the whole company. The unsolicited offers of help abruptly stopped at this point. He felt confident he would continue to be dominant and he was calling his own shots. This is very off-putting to others to say the least. His manager pulled him aside and said, "I'm excited you're doing well, but we expect you to culturally fit in as well. My concern is you're starting to create an atmosphere that isn't the kind we have here, so tone down some of the predictions and bragging and focus in on your progress." Alan responded, "I see what you're trying to do, but you don't have to worry about me. I know I can come on strong, but I'm a good guy."

Then came week two of month two, and Alan didn't get any sales, which is actually hard to do. His manager called him in and said let's talk, you had a rough week. Now Alan, a little frustrated, reassured his manager that it's just a slump and maybe a little bad luck. It wasn't on him—just the circumstances.

By the next week, Alan broke his shutout streak but not by much. In an organization where the average was 8.5 sales per week, he had 3. He was now settling into the lower third of the company after his big first week. As you can imagine, those who were back on top of the sales board gave Alan a little ribbing to the effect of, "I thought you were going to break all the records?" That got frustrating for Alan, and created some conflicts, all while his production continued to sputter.

The manager pulled him aside and said I know I don't have to worry, but I'm getting a little worried. From a relationship and production standpoint, you're having some trouble. Let's do what we should have done in the first place. Let's listen to some calls together and get you back on track. You're talented, this should be a breeze. Alan said I'm doing what I've always done, and it works because I'm good at it.

As the manager is attempting to steer him right, he continued the *don't have to worry about me* mantra. By the end of that month, he was under the minimum standard.

Starting out the third month in much the same way, by this point, his manager had no desire to continue to try to help him. He wasn't contributing to the bottom line, so the manager was looking for results or a resignation. By the end of month 3, Alan ended up below again, and then put himself out of his misery and quit the job.

In the time that he was there, over the three-month transitional period, he did less than Michelle. He diminished the culture and quit right after the 90-day point. This wasn't a devious plan by Alan to go through the interview, get hired, go through training, and then spend two months failing (after one month thinking he was better than he was).

The game plan was for him to find a job to make the money he wanted to make and enjoy doing it. But he didn't bring the right attitude to the party. He was offered help time and time again but didn't want it. He made no inroads from a support structure standpoint and just caused a general bad feeling in the sales environment. I don't think that was Alan's goal. He would have much preferred for this to be successful. But when you reject others' help, and you don't lift up the people around you, you can expect for the transition not to work.

In an alternate universe, he might not have had that early slump and figured it out from the jump. But guess what? That early slump is so common that we're even devoting an entire chapter to it. When we get there, you'll see that when that happens, how you act in those early weeks in the sales environment and with your team is so important for helping you navigate that early struggle so you don't fall apart all alone on an island like Alan.

TRANSITIONAL TAKEAWAYS

Hopefully this chapter imparted the idea that though the training portion of the job is over, the learning portion is still in its infancy. This is no time to take your foot off the gas. It's time to double down, realign your attitude for this new challenge, and be diligent and organized so that your early time on the sales floor is successful. At the beginning we celebrated, so we're going to end the chapter on a slightly different note–with a warning.

In your first few months on the sales floor at a new job, it's on you to lay a foundation for long-term success. If you're leaving it up to your organization to structure your time and your effort so that you can be successful, you run a huge risk of that never coming to fruition. You need to take ownership of this part of the journey and keep your attitude as positive as can be. If you can do that, you're going to make it through this transition with flying colors.

Hopefully, after you've made it through your first 90 days, you'll even send me a Twitter DM or email telling me your story so that I can include it in a future edition of this book. I would love nothing more than to hear that you stuck to the program and knocked it out of the park because I know from experience that this works. And, to be honest, it's not rocket science.

The steps are simple, but they do require a good attitude, focused attention, and constant effort.

Good luck at your first days and weeks on the sales floor and get ready for the next chapter.

Motivational Mantra:
"Maximize your talent, minimize your learning curve, and enlist mentors who can help.

GET-TO-WORK WORKSHEET

Exercise 1: Sales Call Checklist

When you review your sales interactions, make sure that you're doing the following:

- ❏ Did I set an agenda for the call?
- ❏ Did I develop the customer's needs?
- ❏ Did I present the product as a specific solution to those needs?
- ❏ Did I ask for the business?
- ❏ If there was an objection, did I respond in an educational manner that would lead to a redirection toward the sale?

If you answered no to any of the above questions, you don't have to beat yourself up. It's simple going to help you make improvement going forward.

SIX

Getting Over the First Sales Slump

SLUMPS CAN COME in a lot of different shapes and sizes and can be caused by different circumstances. The amount of pressure you'll feel during a slump when you're starting out is much higher than one when you're already established as a top performer. This chapter will cover:

1. What a slump is, and why it happens
2. The effects of a sales slump
3. Tried and true ways to get out of a slump as quickly as possible

The strategies you'll learn will be applicable for any rough patch you may encounter in your career, but more specifically, it will help you deal with that very first sales slump you'll have in a new position.

What exactly is a slump?

At its core, a slump is when the results that you are achieving are no longer in line with the talent and effort that you're putting in. You're working hard, doing what you assume to be all the right things, and you have talent–but the results just aren't there.

There are a lot of reasons why you might find yourself in a slump. Generally, it comes down to the effectiveness of the process you're using, your confidence level, and the amount of energy you have.

I would caution that just because you have a rough interaction or two, doesn't mean you're in a slump. You can blow a sale and not be in a slump. Everyone can take their eye off the ball, but you can shake that off. But once feelings of doubt and frustrations start to swell, that's when you're in a slump and when I would suggest you implement this process in order to get out.

The Most Common Reason for a Slump

When you find yourself getting into a slump, it's usually because you've lost focus in whatever your process is. When that happens, you start to do things that take you further and further away from the successful parts of the process. In trying to help so many people overcome a sales slump, I've listened in on their interactions and it's always striking how far away they had gotten from their process.

You might wonder, why would someone move away from the sales process that they trained to learn, especially if they had early success with it? It comes back to comfort. When things get challenging, people have a tendency to revert back to things they used to do that were more comfortable.

Think about it this way. When you're executing a sales process properly, it should act as a filtration system. You take a prospective customer and walk them through a lot of doors that will ultimately lead them to a sale. Some things in that process might not be comfortable. You might have to get a little personal when you're working on needs development. A lot of times they are going to push back against probing questions and that's uncomfortable. Because we maybe don't trust the process yet, to avoid that negative feeling, we might start softening our approach. Instead of developing needs, we move into giving a presentation of product features and benefits rather than follow the process that filters out the non-purchasers from the purchasers. It feels easier that way, but it comes with a price.

When you start corkscrewing your process to make it more comfortable for the nonbuyers, it means you're not going to be doing enough to earn the buyers. You're going to have a lot of people who would say you've been very helpful with the wonderful information you've given them, but they're not going to have enough emotional content to consummate an actual sale. Your process is no longer a filtration process–it has become a commercial for your product. That's not going to be enough to take the people who need your product as a solution over the finish line. You avoided conflict throughout the process, so when you ask for the sale, it's not anchored in their situation enough for them to say yes. That is the most common reason for a slump.

A Closer Look at the Sales Process

If you want to excel in sales, there are things you must do every time you perform.

Needs development. You need to develop your customer's needs for the product. Your customer must understand the consequences of not purchasing your solution, and it's up to you as the high integrity sales expert to explain how to solve that problem. But you

can't just make that up. You can't impose needs. You have to ask the right set of questions to get them to tell you.

A slump sign: When salespeople are in a slump, establishing needs is generally the first thing you discover that is missing or soft. They might ask a few cursory questions, but nothing of substance.

The solution. The next step in the process is to present your product as a specific solution to their specific needs. If you already did not get down into the weeds with the client to find out their problems, that will make it impossible to present your product as a customized solution.

A slump sign: Slumping salespeople end up sharing generic

features of the product, but those might be irrelevant if they don't match the customer's actual needs.

Asking for the sale. If you do not ask for the sale or some action from the client to purchase the product, you're literally missing the most important thing in sales. Yet, I've heard countless sales interactions where there is no ask. The reason is that it's hard to ask for something when you don't think you deserve it. On a subconscious level, if you haven't developed needs and offered the product as a solution in the right way, you know deep down you didn't earn the right to ask for the business.

A slump sign: If someone is just throwing out the price and then going back into features, or they just let it hang out there until the customer says they'll get back to you, you may be in a slump. Because the sales rep is getting an objection they're not prepared for, it's difficult to overcome. In fact, the customer isn't even really objecting because you didn't actually ask for anything.

Responding to the objection. If you get a no, you may want to schedule a time to get back in touch and hope for the best. You already swung and missed, and now you're trying to do something much harder–get a customer you didn't handle properly the first time to change their mind. In the meantime, they've probably gone and talked to your competitors.

Slump sign: In most cases, after chasing for a while, you'll hear back that they decided to go in another direction.

The Effects of a Sales Slump

Sales slumps are more challenging than having a drought in other fields. When baseball players are in a hitting slump, they're making the same money. But in sales, it's a little more frustrating because not only does struggling not feel good, but you're probably making less money as a result. It can also add a lot of pressure if you're just starting out and haven't started earning commission yet. Plus, if you haven't endeared yourself to management in a substantial enough way, you probably haven't earned any leeway or sense of job security.

Add to that the fact that you're working a new process that you're not fully confident in yet and selling new products that you don't fully understand. You're in a new atmosphere where you want to establish yourself as someone who can be counted on. Financially, you're looking to get back on track. It can feel downright devastating when you have even one really bad day. But as that day turns into three or four, or two weeks, it's going to start to build. As your frustration level goes up, two big things happen: your motivation level goes down and your confidence goes down. And thus, a vicious cycle has started.

Salespeople can take a ton more rejection than most people, but if you get a lot of yesses along the way, it doesn't matter. When you're not getting the yesses, though, it's hard to keep up that same level of enthusiasm and some self-doubt will start to slip in.

You might think: Maybe this job isn't for me. You might then become disengaged, and every time you begin an interaction, you're already deflated and defeated before you start.

If it's been a week or two and you're below your minimum standard or the company's, it's only natural to start doubting whether or not you can do this. Or, you might start questioning the process, or pointing the finger at the manager, the leads, or a tiny humming sound that your phone makes. No matter the case, you're uncomfortable and your energy and confidence levels have plummeted.

The good news is, this slump shall pass...if you know what to do.

Breaking the Slump

You might not believe it yet, but there are three things you can do that will absolutely, unequivocally get you out of your sales slump. Are you ready? Follow this three-part checklist and I promise you; you can send your slump packing.

1. Analyze your sales process.

If you look at the four parts of the sales process–needs development, offering the product as a solution for specific needs, asking for the sale, and then responding to the objections–each one needs to be good enough. So, if you were being graded on a scale of 1 to 10 (10 being you're the best salesperson ever), you should be at around a 7 on each part if you want to achieve a reasonable level of sales success. This is where having mentors and doing comparisons of your sales interactions can be very helpful. If you have recordings of your phone sales, you can request to hear a successful call and then look at the differences.

Your team leader can really help here by listening in with you to try to pinpoint where you're not up to that level-7 proficiency. The key is that you need to figure out what you aren't doing well, but also *why* you aren't doing it well.

The number one question I ask when I'm coaching others is: "What is the least comfortable portion of the sales interaction for you right now?" This helps provide a clue as to where you might need to tweak your process. They might say when I ask questions, they get short with me and it's hard to get back on track. Translation: That could mean they've stopped developing needs because it's uncomfortable.

Once you know what you're doing and why, you have to remind yourself (or your sales leader can help remind you), that if a customer doesn't know why they need your product, no information beyond that is going to be relevant for them, and you're wasting your time.

In fact, you have to get through all of the non-negotiable portions of a sale no matter how uncomfortable they are. The more you do it, the easier it will get. Generally, if you figure out the customer's need for that product and you offer a solution for that need, you should have a little more confidence asking for the sale.

Each step builds toward the next, and that is going to help you tremendously. Once you get to the point where you ask for action from the customer, you know they're either going to take action, ask more questions, or object. The objection is the only thing you have to be prepared for in an empathetic and educational manner to help the customer understand what the world looks like with and without your product. And it's much easier to do that if you know it's coming.

Let's fast forward and assume you had issues with one or even all of these four steps. If you can recommit to each step, you'll at least have solved the process portion of your slump.

2. Rebuild your confidence.

When your confidence is shaken, even when you're doing the right things, it can give your customer pause. If you're not sure of yourself, your customer is going to translate that to you not being sure of the solution you're offering. If you seem unsure, they're not going to think, gee, maybe you're having a crisis of confidence. Instead, 100% of the time, they will think that you don't believe in the solution, or in the solution for them. And *that's* the kiss of death for sales. Unfortunately, depending on the length of your slump, your confidence can be very banged up.

To get your confidence back, you have to go through a simple exercise. Ask yourself what you do feel confident in and create a list of things. Start with the company you work for. Are you confident that the company is doing the right things and offering products that people want to buy? That answer should be yes. (If your answer is no to that, go back to the portion of the book about picking the right job for you.) Assuming you have confidence in the company, now you have your foundation.

Next, take it a step further and ask yourself: has the company done a good job finding leaders to run the company who can develop sales processes and train new salespeople so they can have success in selling this product? If your peers are successful, and you have had some success, that answer should also be yes.

From there, ask yourself: does this sales process work when executed properly? You should be able to look around at the sales team and answer yes to that.

Finally, it's time to turn inward. Answer this: Am I confident that I can execute this sales process effectively? Again, you don't need to be the best salesperson in the world. You just have to be sure you can execute this process. And you should! You learned it in your training, and you've had success with it in your early weeks on the job. So now you have a successful company, a competent leadership team, an effective process, and a belief in yourself that even when all else fails, you can still follow your process. Once you realize all that, you're on your way toward rebuilding your confidence.

3. Restore your energy.

Sales in its raw form is a transfer of energy. The bad news is when you're in a slump, your energy, for lack of a better word, sucks. You're drained, and that state of mind is not going to inspire someone to take action. The last step for getting out of your slump is to find a way to manufacture your energy. No, that doesn't mean drinking five red bulls.

It means focusing on your body posture, your tone of voice, and putting a smile on your face. Make sure you're projecting. It might feel like you're faking it at first, but you want to act like you have enthusiasm. Now that you've dug back into your process to make any corrections, and regained confidence in your ability to execute that process, it's time to get pumped up.

If you don't think this is a big deal, allow me to share this quick anecdote.

I once knew a salesperson who was so good, but he hit a wall. He was the kind of person who was proactive in finding a solution for himself to the point where he was probably even overthinking it a bit. He came to me for help, so I listened in and his process was fine. His confidence was a little shook, but what really stood out to me was his low energy level. This was someone who usually had a 10,000-megawatt smile and voice, and he was at about 2,000. I asked him to meet me the next day before his shift.

We went into a side huddle room, and I had my phone with earbuds ready for him. He popped them in his ears, and I played for him the Wu Tang Clan's C.R.E.A.M. (Cash Rules Everything Around

Me). I made him listen to the whole thing. Once it finished, I took my phone back, opened the door, and left without saying a word. He went onto the sales floor, and he was pumped up. It clicked for him, and he was out of his slump almost immediately. All he needed to do was readjust his energy.

I knew this would work for him, because it was something that I learned early on when I had a sales slump. I remember telling a colleague of mine during a smoking break why I was so frustrated, and he gave me the most casual response. He said, "If you're doing everything right and you're not getting sales, it's your energy level." And he walked away. And I thought, damn—could that really be it?

I smacked my cheeks a little, splashed some water on my face, and got back at it with a higher level of energy. And son of a you-know-what... I was right back on track!

The lesson: Energy is not something to be taken lightly when trying to get over a sales slump. A lot of times just slamming your foot down on the gas can help you get back to that high level of enthusiasm you had right out of training. In a lot of cases, it's the easiest thing to fix, but you have to recognize that it's the problem.

Just as you went through your sales process above, you want to do a regular check on your energy level—even on a daily basis. This can not only help you get out of a slump, but it can help prevent you from getting into one at all. When you maintain a high energy level, your customers feed off of it and might push back less, and in turn, that allows you to maintain some confidence.

So, there you have it. If you are in a slump, you might have to tweak your process, and address your confidence and energy levels. Do those three things, and it's all you'll ever need to do.

One caveat: Getting out of your slump doesn't mean you're going to land your next 10 sales in a row. It's still a numbers game, and you're still going to encounter people who are not the right fit for your product. Don't let that discourage you. Or worse—don't revert right back into the bad process or low levels of confidence and energy that caused your slump. Just know that if you follow the steps above, you will recover, even if it doesn't happen instantly.

A Word on Self Love

Salespeople are very tough, but when slumps happen, there is a huge tendency to kick yourself into oblivion. Just like we discussed in the training chapter, you have to be patient with yourself. You have to be your best internal cheerleader and learn to tune out the critic.

A slump is not an indictment of you as a human being or your value to the world. It happens to the best of us, but you'll definitely recover more quickly if you don't waste precious energy kicking your own butt.

I've seen dozens of people who weren't ever able to recover from an early sales slump. They never got on track and they didn't like losing every day and feeling bad about themselves, so they quit. Or they kept showing up to the job defeated, and inevitably let nature take its course and got fired.

If you're feeling down, you need to remind yourself of all the amazing steps you've taken to get to this point. Plus, getting over this final hurdle–your first sales slump–means your transition is just about complete. Don't let all of your hard work go to waste because you were too hard on yourself. You can't control how the world treats you, but you can love yourself.

You've been through a lot and when a slump happens, just remember that you have all of the tools, training, and experience you need to get through it. You've never been more prepared to get out of a slump than you are right now. And when you come back out on top, you'll be all the more equipped for success.

TRANSITIONAL TAKEAWAYS

Now that we understand where slumps come from, how to recognize where they are coming from, and what we can do to get out of them, you're at a point where you should be able to overcome any sales slump you encounter. That should be a great feeling. The first one can leave you with more doubt than any others you will face, but now that you're armed with the information to successfully navigate them, your transition into this new job is nearly complete.

Once you overcome that first sales slump, all the hardest parts are done. For that, you should be tremendously proud. Take a couple of hours upon finishing this chapter to reward yourself for getting this far, because you deserve it.

Congratulations!

Up next: You'll take the final step toward completing your transition into a new sales career.

Motivational Mantra:
"Slumps happen, but know this: You've never been more prepared to get out of a slump than you are right now."

GET-TO-WORK WORKSHEET

Slumpbuster Checklist

Sales Process

Needs Development	1-2-3-4-5-6-7-8-9-10
Presenting Solution	1-2-3-4-5-6-7-8-9-10
Asking For Business	1-2-3-4-5-6-7-8-9-10
Responding to Objections	1-2-3-4-5-6-7-8-9-10

Confidence

Do you believe in your company?	Yes / No
Do you believe in your management team?	Yes / No
Do you believe the sales process works?	Yes / No
Do you believe in your ability to execute the sales process?	Yes / No

Energy

What is your current energy level?	1-2-3-4-5-6-7-8-9-10
Are you projecting?	Yes / No
Is your posture strong?	Yes / No
Are you smiling?	Yes / No

Moving Past The Transition

When I moved to Los Angeles, I arrived at LAX with five duffle bags and three grand, less the cost of a coffee and croissant. I knew no one, had no job, no place to live...nothing. It was quite possibly the worst plan ever. Within a week, I moved out of my weekly rental into an apartment with a roommate I had just met. After about a month, I started a job as a waiter at a pizza place. I remember coming home after my first week on the job. I had money coming in and a roof over my head. I knew I had made it through the hardest part. I bought a six pack of beer and toasted with my 70+ year old roommate, Ella (whole other story). I hope your plan was better than mine.

SEVEN

Settling in and Staying Passionate

YOU DID IT! You successfully transitioned into your new sales job. You dealt with all the pitfalls. You sacrificed professionally, financially, and emotionally in order to achieve the job and career that you deserve. And you have my heartfelt congratulations!

As a reminder, this book was written with the intention of accompanying you through the sales transition step by step. However, even if you're reading this prior to transitioning and don't quite relate at the moment, know that the same congratulations will be waiting here for you when you get through your own transition someday.

Now that you've taken a moment to celebrate your success, it's time to get back to it. You might be at the end of your 90-day transition period, but you're still at the very beginning of your new job. As you settle in, there's a chance that having gone through the emotionally charged period you just went through, you might feel a bit of let down or a loss of passion as things level out.

While that's normal, if you allow this period of calm to develop into disengagement, that could have a negative impact on your success. This chapter is designed to serve as a warning, as well as provide some strategies for maintaining a healthy level of passion as you continue along in your career.

So here you are–about 6 months to one year into your new job, and things have become mundane. The thrill and excitement of the newness has worn off, and you might find yourself noticing flaws in the systems, getting nitpicky with your coworkers, and even beginning to dread certain tasks. While that's all normal, and you can't be enthusiastic 24/7, it's on you to seek out ways to stay excited and engaged because as a salesperson, it's a requirement for success. Luckily, there are a number of simple ways to do that, and the rest of this chapter will show you how.

1. Keep Learning.

You might be seeing wonderful results from executing the sales process, which is great. But once you reach a level of mastery, you might start to go on autopilot. And that part of you that craves educational nourishment might feel neglected. That's why if you want to stay passionate and continue to improve in your job, you have to keep learning.

The good news is that learning can happen in a vast number of ways. It can happen through books like this, via employer-sponsored training programs, formal continuing education, coaching sessions with mentors, seminars, and more. It can be as simple as watching a series of YouTube videos or reading industry magazine articles. Learning opportunities are all around if you have a desire to learn.

I firmly believe that there's no such thing as a plateau in sales. You are always in one of two states: a salesperson who is improving or one who is getting worse. For those getting better, it's because they are continuing to feed new ideas into the machine.

A Lesson from the Stage

Indulge me as I share with you some insight I've learned as a comedian that translates pretty well into a sales environment. In a stand-up act, if you have a series of bits that you do over and over again, it can work really well and get lots of laughs. You've gone through the work and your act is good and audiences will react favorably to it. But something else happens when you keep doing the same act without injecting anything new. What you're going to see is that even though people are laughing in the right places, the response will get a little less enthusiastic each time. It takes a long time to notice this from the stage, but after a while, you'll realize the laughs aren't as big as they used to be.

What's the deal? The jokes are the same. They're still funny, right? But what actually happens is because you've done the set so many times, you no longer have to think about it. It's become habit. It's more like you're doing an impression of yourself doing your act. So, yes, it still works, but it doesn't work to the degree it used to because it's lacking that energy and excitement that you had when you first started doing the act. When you were still feeling out the audience and testing new bits for the first time, you were more curious, more engaged, and more in tune to what was going on around you.

In sales, it works very much the same way. As you master the sales process, you know what works, so you're going to ask the same questions, and largely get the same responses. Once you're doing it on instinct, it's a comfortable feeling. But it also lacks that tiny bit of fear of the unknown that I think is crucial to sales success–as well as comedy. The way to fix this is to continue to learn about new ideas and techniques and try new things. When you do that, there is something magical that happens.

If I do a 30-minute comedy routine but add a new two-minute joke, there is a tremendous amount of unknown in those two minutes. There's excitement, anticipation, and hopefulness all wrapped up together that resonates throughout the whole show. It gets me into the moment and winds up freshening up the entire routine. It makes the entire 30 minutes feel alive.

The big takeaway: If you add a new element from something you've learned into the thing you've mastered; you can continuously improve and keep things exciting–whether you're on stage or in the sales forum.

It might be one small attempt at engaging in a customer's concerns, but that one thing is going to create an emotional environment where you're alive and thinking and even a little worried that it's not going to work, and it will keep you on your toes and create a deeper connection with your client. Give it a try and let me know how it goes.

2. Reimagine your goals

By now, you might have achieved some goals that you set out to conquer, whether it was landing that first sale, or hitting a specific number in your first few months. If so, it's time to get out the whiteboard and start over. In any job and even in your personal life, it's important to always keep resetting the bar so you have something to work toward.

With sales goals, there's always a tendency to use numbers, and that makes a lot of sense since they are easy to track. But what I would suggest is that you go beyond the numbers to make sure there are other aspects to your goals that have greater meaning to you. Try anchoring numbers-based goals to something tangible in your life. So instead of just saying you want to sell $100,000 of products this month, take it a step further to say you want to earn $5,000 in commission for those sales. Even further than that, link it to a financial goal you have: I want to pay off $5,000 on the credit card I ran up during my sales transition. Now *that's* something meaningful to set your sights on!

You'll now have an emotional investment that can get you through the tough days.

Of course, you can set additional goals that aren't dollar-driven, too. Maybe you want to become a team leader at the end of 90 days, too. Your goals should be specific to your own desires.

No matter what type of goal you set, the first thing to keep in mind is to use the SMART acronym to make sure your goal is: Specific, Measurable, Achievable, Relevant, and Time-based. That will help ensure that you're not setting the bar too low or too high.

Finally, think about the timing. Goals can come in all shapes and sizes, and many experts recommend having both short- and long-term goals. What I recommend for this particular phase of your career is that shorter goals may be easier to stay on course with. If you only set a 10-year goal, it's going to be tough to stay accountable to that, and it's a long wait. Who knows how your motivations and desires will change in that time period? Instead (or in addition to your long-term vision), I recommend coming up with 30-, 60-, and 90-day plans. Those are timelines that you can wrap your mind around. It's never too far off that it will become irrelevant in your day-to-day. As you get further into your career, longer and longer goals will make more sense. But at this stage, try to keep it a little more bite-sized so you can allow yourself some flexibility along the way. Remember, you're still fairly new in the job–you don't really have a grasp on what's possible or what the limits of your capabilities are. As you get a better understanding of the job, it will be much easier to adjust your goals when they are shorter in nature.

3. Take advantage of everything your job has to offer.

Depending upon the size of the company, there could be a lot of extra perks that go along with the job, from a gym membership to programs offered to enrich your life, to social activities. Do your best to find out what programs and extras are offered by your job, and even if it was something that you never thought you'd do, give it a try.

Participation will not only keep the working experience fresh, but it also helps you feel good about where you're working and allows you to interact with your coworkers in new ways. Those kinds of experiences can enrich and build your relationships so you're not just coming into work to do your job, but also because you've built bonds with your coworkers who make it a joy to come in each day.

If your job is sponsoring an outing to see a baseball game and you don't love baseball, no one is forcing you to go. But then again, it could give you the opportunity to see your associates in a new light. Chances are you're going to have fun while having a shared experience outside the office. There's a reason why companies sponsor these types of things.

Of course, if you work for a smaller firm there might not be as much to take advantage of, but you can try to start something. Try to spearhead an initiative. Explore what the neighborhood around your office has to offer and invite coworkers to come along. If your coworkers are in a band or part of a theater group, support them. Go see a show. When you go back to work on Monday and everyone is talking about the outing on Friday, you won't feel left out. All of these efforts create anchors to your new job and help to create an atmosphere where you can feel comfortable, and take your shoes off, so to speak (don't really take off your shoes!).

Final thought: My grandmother used to say, "If you're ever bored, it's your own fault!" And she was right. It's up to you to keep things interesting by taking advantage of what's offered or taking the initiative to get something started.

4. Be active in any committees or projects going on at work.

Again, it's about deepening your investment and highlighting your greater purpose in the organization. If there are any sort of ongoing committees asking for volunteers, put in some time. I've seen that it's often the Achilles heel of salespeople that they don't ever want to leave the sales environment, and what ends up happening is they burn out.

Sometimes contributing in a way other than your sales output can be just the thing to keep things exciting, and it can actually boost your sales numbers if you can ride the wave of that enthusiasm.

Plus, being involved in or taking on company projects means that you have a chance to assert your own influence into the organization. At the same time, your management team will take notice that you're someone who wants to invest time and energy into the organization beyond your job description. That's the kind of thing that gets mentioned during internal interviews about promotion candidates, or perhaps during your annual review. Yes, you need to keep your sales numbers up, too, but you become a more valuable employee overall when you participate.

If you work for a smaller firm without these kinds of committees, take some initiative and start something. Maybe you can suggest putting together a core group with representatives from different departments to keep the culture strong or focus on office safety. If you notice a problem, that's the perfect time to start a problem-solving committee. If you show you have pride in your company and the leadership ability to start a project and see it through to the end, you'll become more than just the guy who gets the sales.

5. Gamification

Sales games and contests are designed to keep things fun and add a level of friendly competition among the salespeople. You don't have to take it too seriously especially if you're in competition with colleagues as you certainly don't want it to create friction or harm relationships. But since salespeople generally have thicker skin, if a little friendly trash talk is something you and your colleagues are OK with, it can keep everyone motivated to achieve better results. So, don't ever be too cool for a management-sponsored game. Whether there are ways to earn additional rewards or if it's just for bragging rights, it's a fun way to keep everyone engaged.

If there isn't anything like that at your company, you can create your own sales games or personal challenges to keep the job interesting day in and day out. You can try to beat your own high score or partner up with a sales buddy. Maybe the challenge is to see who can get the first sale of the day, or who can get the most before lunch. No matter the game, the idea is to keep it fun.

TRANSITIONAL TAKEAWAYS

There are a lot of things you can do to keep your job interesting and stay enthused and engaged, even if you're at a point where you have the job down pat and are achieving results. That doesn't mean every day and every task is going to be the most exciting thing ever. But it's your responsibility to make sure that if you're in the job you wanted to be in, that you do what you can to keep it exciting for yourself. That means:

1. Keep learning
2. Reset your goals
3. Take advantage of what's offered for you
4. Get involved and deepen your relationships
5. Keep it fun

And if you still come upon a few boring days or start to see some flaws, think back to the nail-biting and hand-wringing that came before when you were first starting out. You made it through that tough transition, so don't judge the aftermath too harshly.

There's a lot you can do at this stage of the game to make the most out of every day. Don't be afraid to make a major investment in yourself and your company because that's the only way you're going to get a major return.

Motivational Mantra:
"If you're ever bored, it's your own fault. Find the fun in what you do."

GET-TO-WORK WORKSHEET

Keep the Passion Alive Scorecard

Give yourself 1 point for every checkmark – and try to get to six or above.
This month, I'm going to keep things exciting by:

- ❏ subscribing to a daily podcast
- ❏ signing up for an online webinar
- ❏ going to a work-sponsored seminar or training
- ❏ attending an industry conference
- ❏ reading books (you get an automatic check once you finish this book!)
- ❏ setting new goals for myself
- ❏ attending a company outing or event
- ❏ doing something social with coworkers
- ❏ joining a workplace committee or project
- ❏ playing or creating a sales game

EIGHT

Giving Back to Move Forward

YOU'VE COMPLETED your transition and have probably been in your role for quite some time now. Yet... there's still more of this book left. I can assure you that I'm not trying to make this book any longer than it needs to be. In fact, I've gone through great pains to make sure it's as short and actionable as possible. I hope you've found that to be the case.

That said, I do have just a little more to talk about. I'd like to offer a little more insight on my greatest joy that happened to be the result of one of the toughest transitions of my career. I hope it fully impresses upon you that some unintended good things can come out of a transition. For me, it allowed me to learn that leading others and giving back was my calling, something I would have never learned had I not gone through a pretty uncomfortable transition.

My Biggest Transition

After having appeared on multiple TV episodes on shows like *My Name is Earl*, *Weeds*, and *Jimmy Kimmel Live*, I found myself in a position where I needed to go make some actual money. So, I returned to my sales management position with a small privately owned specialty insurance company in the San Fernando valley.

I noticed that the time away (or maybe it was the bright lights of Hollywood?) changed my perspective, and I approached the management position a little bit differently. I was much more concerned with helping the sales reps get better rather than my own personal accolades.

Upon my return, I identified a few salespeople who I hadn't known before and really committed to making sure they would get all of the benefits of my experience in that industry as well as my encouragement. For the first time in a long time, I fell in love with what I was doing outside of entertainment. Every small win for my reps was a big win for me. I settled into a position where the money was great, and my team was functioning really well–it was satisfying and fulfilling for me.

About three months into it, the rest of my management team and I were summoned into the owner's office. We knew the business we were in was fledgling, but we all had a sense of security based on our solid sales numbers. The owner began that he had good news and bad news to share.

The good news was that we had the opportunity to start up a brand-new specialty insurance division within a publicly traded company. The mood in the room was one of surprise, but also excitement. Then came the bad news. The company we were currently working for was going immediately bankrupt the next day and couldn't even cover the payroll or sales commission for the last two weeks. Just like that, excitement and surprise turned to shock and uncertainty.

We were then told that it was our task to inform the next layer of management, and after that, the entire sales team. With barely any time to process this news ourselves, we called a meeting with the first group, and it was met with anger. A couple of team members even stormed out of the room. It was a humbling experience to say the least.

Knowing that I had at least a month of financial struggle ahead of me, I tried to look past that to see the possibilities on the horizon. This new corporate entity had a good benefits package, the pay was fair, and I'd have access to the kind of resources that I'd never had before to change an industry and do things the way I always wanted to do them.

Knowing that I'd be informing the entire sales team about these developments the next day, I thought carefully about how to frame this news to them. I believed my purpose was to help as many others as possible see past the temporary shock and anger and attempt to shepherd them along this new journey with me.

As a professional comedian, having a room full of people to talk to was a comfortable situation for me, but this was hardly a time for jokes. I had to be direct, candid, and do my best to wear my heart on my sleeve and let them know how I felt about the upcoming opportunity.

If I'm being frank, it was the most uncomfortable meeting of my entire career, and it resulted in about half of the sales team walking out forever. But for the other half, I was confident that I had steered them toward a position in which they could be successful.

We got started right away building our team from the ground up. We didn't even have office space for the first month and had to create every system and process from scratch.

Somewhere through that process of being a little financially strapped and working harder than I ever worked before, I gained a sense of ownership over my career. I began to harness my power to influence and lead others, and it gave me a tremendous sense of gratification. I also experienced some doubt, thinking I was unworthy and not prepared to meet this challenge.

I decided to embrace this transition into a leadership role and began to read and devour as much material on leadership and whatever process I was working on. I decided that I needed to become a career learner so I could always be at my best.

As the weeks went on, we started developing a culture, we started to grow the team, and we started succeeding. One of the reps who came over from the original company was now one of my top reps at this new company. That's when the light bulb turned on for me that this was something I could do. I realized I was actually capable of helping people improve their careers and their lives.

This, to me, equaled true success. I had already achieved many of the things that my younger self defined as success, from being on TV, to having people applaud my comedy, and of course, making a good living. But it was not until that moment when this company really started flourishing and the people who trusted in me were actually seeing their hard work come to fruition that I fully realized what success really felt like.

Why am I telling you this? It's so that you understand that there is a level of gratification beyond your sales numbers. And while leadership and giving back might not be for everybody, I felt compelled to share this story for those of you reading this book to whom this message will resonate. And hopefully, it may even potentially alter the course of your career in a good way someday.

The Benefits of Giving Back

When you decide to be a leader or mentor to others, there is actually a lot in it for you, too. For starters, you'll never be alone again. Most of us have experienced a time in our career where we felt totally isolated, but once you go down the path of being a leader to others, it opens doors that can never be closed to you again. The people who you help will always be a source of affirmation and joy to you. They will reach out to you for advice, or to thank you. They may even have a desire to follow you wherever you go. And that, my friends, is an indescribable feeling.

If you go down this path, you will be building a community that will live on and create a true legacy.

In sales, money is always a driver for success, but that joy is fleeting. What lasts a lot longer is when people develop a deep appreciation for your contributions to their life. You never hear a eulogy where someone says, "I remember in April 2006, he made so much money." Instead, you will hear someone talk about how without that person's influence, they wouldn't be who they are today.

If you are a high achieving salesperson who wants to sell the most and break records, I applaud you, and I'm not suggesting that you should stop being motivated by that. What I am saying is someone will inevitably break your record, but the impact you have on those around you can never be taken away or forgotten.

You may be wondering what leadership or mentorship has to do with a book on sales transitions, so let me tie it all together for you.

1. **Your transition experience might inspire you to pay it forward.** In writing this book, the number one outcome I would like to see is that you not only have a successful transition, but that you can use that experience to shepherd others through an uncomfortable time in their career. It is my hope that upon reading this, that from here on out, you'll always be on the lookout for someone to mentor or help guide much like I hope this book has helped you.

2. **Spend your time on those who not only *need* your help, but those who sincerely *want* it.** The chances of someone actually taking your advice will be much higher if the person is self-aware and open to ideas. Don't waste your energy on someone who doesn't realize they can use a helping hand.

3. **Helping others is good for your career, too.** While you should want to help others for its own sake, an ancillary benefit is that management will notice. Whenever I look to move someone into a management role, one of the first things I look at is how helpful this person has been to others. If they haven't been willing to support others, then I know as a manager they will be less effective in leading their team.

At some point, you're going to be faced with a decision where you can either take a minute to help someone or decline to help them so you can focus on yourself. As an individual performer in a sales role, you can't spend all of your time helping others, but when you can dig deep even in those moments when you'd rather not, others will see that it actually means something to you to be helpful to them. That will build some of those bonds that I've talked about.

It's important to understand that what I'm suggesting is not about trying for a positional change toward a management role. When I talk about leadership, it's about how you conduct yourself, not about a particular job title. It's a skill and a way of life to be applied wherever you are in the organization. You can be a leader in an entry level position. Leadership knows no bounds when it's done from a place of actual care for the people you're leading, or to promote the success of the organization.

The Easiest Way to Give Back? Give This Book Away

This may come as a surprise, but if you get something from this book, I don't want you to tell people to go buy it. I want you to give this book to someone who needs it. My only request is that instead of asking for it back, you encourage them to pass it on.

I am not looking to make millions of dollars off of this book. I saw a need for it out there, and so I wrote it. Nothing would please me more than to stumble upon a well-worn copy of this book that was passed around to 15 people. So, I encourage you to give it away, even if it means that I don't sell another book. Although my sales numbers might be lower, my career calling will be a step closer to where I want it to be.

Final Thoughts

There's a high percentage chance that you're in the world of sales if you're reading this book, so I'd be willing to bet that you're going to get this next reference. In the movie *Glengarry Glen Ross*, Alec Baldwin gives his famous ABC monologue, "Always be closing."

In that vein, the final thought I want to leave you with is that rather than ABC, remember ABT– "Always be transitioning."

I didn't lie to you when I talked about how long a typical transitional period would take. But I wasn't totally upfront about this fact: **life is one continuous transition.** Not just your career, but in every aspect of your life, you are constantly moving through one transitional period or another. I thought that statement might be a little overwhelming upfront, which is why I saved it for the conclusion of the book.

But when you think about it, the ability to handle transitions is central to everything we do. As a partner, you're transitioning through courting, dating, marriage, becoming parents together, and sometimes, maybe even divorce. Growing up, your relationship with your parents continues to be in a state of transition, going from being totally dependent to counter dependent, to fully independent, to eventually coming full circle where you become their caregiver. As a parent, you know full well that raising a newborn requires different skills than raising a toddler, an 8-year-old, a preteen, a teen, or an adult.

The bottom line is that as a human being, you're continually transitioning from one role to the next, and sometimes, these transitions can happen simultaneously. Although this book is focused on how to transition from one sales position to the next, the lessons learned can be applied to other transitions in your life as well.

At the very least, I'm confident that this book will help you with your sales transitions. But even more than that, I hope that this book has given you the tools to acknowledge all transitions as they are happening, so you can try to bring your best self to each of them.

I invite you to connect with me on social media and tell me your stories, about how this book helped you, as well as what it might be missing. And lastly, I want to say thank you for allowing me to help you along your journey. I appreciate you taking an active role in your own transition, and I hope that it's a successful one.

Motivational Mantra:
"ABT: Always be transitioning."

Acknowledgments

Thank You

This list of people were instrumental in teaching, inspiring, supporting and empowering me. In no particular order, thank you, Dawn Papandrea, Andy Suchan, Joee Suchan, Casey Suchan, Liana Lalli, Paul and Debbie Greco, Kelly Dougherty, Chris and Jill Ficara, Chris Christopherson, Nota Berger, Paul McGee, Brad Basmajian, George Laird, Tranell Montague, Pauline Brooks, Stephanie Lang, Beth Holt, Norm Rosenberg, Jimmy Brogan, Jules DeCruz Mary DeCruz, Frank Lalli, Gail Lalli, Cathy Greco, Grace Greco, Anthony and Nancy Greco, Tim Chizmar, Adam Epstein, Matt Tedesco, Tom D' Intino, Brian Solari, Paul London, TK Matteson, Charles Randle, Raul Rivera, Sergio Castillo, Barry Polterman, Michael and Gina Preston, Michael Fehcter and Kerry Keane.

There are so many more, but this won't be my last book, so for those I missed, it is due to a stressed mind on a deadline, not a lack of appreciation for your impact on my life. Finally, thank you, reader! I know how much you have on your plate and I sincerely appreciate you trusting me with your most valuable commodity: time.

About the Author

Brandon Ficara is an author, acclaimed business advisor, and a thought leader in the areas of sales, business culture, and leadership. Brandon, a Forbes business development contributor, has also had a celebrated stand-up comedy and acting career. He has performed for tens of thousands of people all over the country and been seen by millions on TV on Jimmy Kimmel Live!, My Name is Earl, and Weeds.

Born in Philadelphia, PA and raised in the seasonal beach community of Ocean City, NJ, Ficara now lives in Los Angeles, CA, and he is tolerated by his wife and stepdaughter but beloved by his cats...the dog is ambivalent. Born with Sprangles deformity, a condition that required major back surgery at three years old, Brandon used his unique look and outlook to fuel his insatiable desire to entertain, uplift and lead others.

COMING SOON

FUNNY BUSINESS

When Comedy Successfully Meets Business

BRANDON FICARA

Maverick Vision
PUBLISHING